BIG Stitch
knitting

finding your inner stashionista

Becca Smith

All American **Crafts**
Publishing, Inc.

BIG Stitch *knitting*
finding your inner stashionista

Text © 2008 by Becca Smith
Artwork © 2008 All American Crafts, Inc.

All American Crafts Publishing, Inc.
7 Waterloo Road
Stanhope, NJ 07874
www.allamericancrafts.com

Publisher • **Jerry Cohen**
Chief Executive Officer • **Darren Cohen**
Art Director • **Kelly Albertson**

Editor • **Penelope Taylor**
Technical Editor • **Michael del Vecchio**
Proofreader • **Joanna Feller**

Digital Technician • **Kathleen Govaerts**
Technical Illustrator • **Kathleen Govaerts**

Photographer • **Steve Young for RYA Studios**
Photo Stylist • **Penelope Taylor**
Hair & Makeup • **Diane Marinelli**
       for Cornerstone Salon & Spa
Models •   **Joanna Feller**
           Courtney Schreiber
           Dora Tang

Printed in the USA.

ISBN-13: 978-0-9789513-6-8
ISBN-10: 0-978-9513-6-0
Library of Congress Control Number: 2008927325

Dedication

In memory of Dad, who always played the purse strings with a great big smile. Thanks.

Acknowledgments

The inspiration for this book began when I first saw the ginormous needles created by Rachel John in the United Kingdom. Rachel creates beautiful rugs with 25 to 40 fibers at a time. She calls her work Extreme Knitting©, and we are pleased that we represent her needles on this side of the pond.

Jean Ruben, my mother, knitting partner, and supportive critic has helped enormously with this venture by knitting some of the pieces and helping with many of my experiments – both good and bad. Of course, I would not be involved with any of this if it were not for her.

This project took over several rooms of our home, and in the process my darling and patient husband, Herb, untangled my messes, wrapped roving, and became an expert swifter. Our son, E.B., has been great at demonstrating our needles and projects while drawing crowds at shows.

My dear friend and wonderful partner in art crime, Suzanne Cohan-Lange, lent her ear and creative juices to help me problem solve along the way. She's on the hot side of the color wheel and a perfect foil to me on the cool side. BagSmith stalwarts Janette Higgins, Dora Tang, Jennie Dawes, and Jackie Smith assisted with knitting, crocheting, proofreading, swifting, and generally keeping the BagSmith balls in the air. John Higgins dedicated himself to making the original Extreme Needles© as well as other designs of large crochet hooks and double pointed needles. He is our Needle Man!

Many wonderful fiber people worked with me in selecting yarns and products for different purposes. They include Robin Page from Pagewood Farms, Cindy Fitzgerald of Heart's Desire, Deana Gavioli and Margery Winter of Berroco, Barry Klein of Trendsetter Yarns, Patti Subik of Great Adirondack Yarns, Liz Tekus and Sue Thompson of Fine Points, **Cristine Hines of Artistic Visions,** and Pam Scott of yarnrep.com.

Last, but certainly not least, I want to thank Penelope Taylor, my editor, who has guided me through this process, encouraging me and gently recommending suggestions that have greatly improved this publication, as well as Michael del Vecchio, whose technical editing and imaginative comments were tremendously helpful.

Contents

Introduction

I am a descendant of needle women. My great grandmother, newly arrived in the United States from Romania, supported her family with her needles and hands, mending, sewing, and knitting. No doubt her skills were passed on from her mother or grandmother. Knit and purl stitches, embroidery, and needlepoint skills were transmitted generation to generation like oral histories. While the stitching progressed, the stories, trials, and tribulations of families and friends were sure to be shared.

My grandmother spent countless hours knitting, crocheting, and meticulously working on petit point, needlepoint, and cross stitch projects. Her petit point silhouettes hang proudly in our home. Cherished pieces that she made for my grandfather are in our cedar chest. My mother remembers sweaters that she took apart during the depression so that she could use the yarn for new sweaters or afghans. She shared these passions with my mother.

In that same cedar chest is a purple striped dress my mother made for me when I was about 13 years old. I remember wearing it proudly, knowing that each stitch was a gift from her hands. Looking back, the pieces represent wonderful memories. Years later, my two sisters and I each received a spectacular handmade coat for our fortieth birthdays. I treasure the guidance she gave me when I first picked up needles, and the continued support she gives me today. Some of the pieces in this book were created in her hands.

It is always interesting to discover needle people from other places. Over the years, I have had the great pleasure of attending and selling our products at the Knitting and Stitching Show at the Alexandra Palace in London, England. One year while walking to our booth, I noticed a display of beautiful, thick rugs near an empty chair surrounded by bags of yarn on cones. A petite woman approached me and started to explain her techniques using the largest needles I had ever seen. She was United Kingdom textile artist Rachel John. She had developed large wooden needles that could accommodate multiple strand knitting. Some of

Extreme Rugs by Rachel John. Each one is knitted with Size 50 US (25mm), using 25 fibers simultaneously.

her rugs incorporated up to 45 fibers, all knit together at the same time. Her enthusiasm was contagious, and I caught the bug. I immediately wanted to bring those needles home to work with them.

Rachel's work is impressive. She masterfully uses color, migrating from one hue to the next by changing the thin fibers row by row. Her experimentation with this technique included building tools large enough to accommodate 1,000 strands of yarn, which were pulled up from a balcony, enabling her to knit a large mattress! Generous with her ideas and teachings, Rachel developed some of the techniques that are noted in this book.

BagSmith manufactures Rachel's needles in the United States using basswood, which is a renewable resource and a very lightweight, durable wood. These tools are very easy to use, and this book will explain tips and tricks for making the process enjoyable and fun. Although they may look daunting at first, the needles are very lightweight and the yarn easily moves over them. The Size 50 US (25mm) and Size 35 US (19mm) needles are available in five lengths from 16" (400mm) to 32" (800mm), making small and large projects possible. You will find patterns in the book that specify both sizes, some in the same pattern. Size U (25mm) crochet hooks are also used as well as some smaller needles and hooks. Other manufacturers make large needles and hooks, but most needles on the market in Size 50 US (25mm) or Size 35 US (19mm) are plastic and do not have the length necessary to make large projects.

Choosing fibers to work with in a world of fabulous textures and delicious colors is my idea of a great time. In this book, you will find a wide range of fibers: inexpensive to expensive, plain and sparkly, bold and subdued. Many of the patterns can be adapted for other yarns, some of which you may be able to find in your stash. Several projects identify the yarns used in the photographs. Other projects use more generic fibers. Use these patterns as guidelines. Adapt them as you wish. As a teacher, I always developed lesson plans, but my most inspiring time in the classroom came when the time was right to throw the lesson plans out.

Enjoy the journey and the process – let's get started!

Becca

"A work of art is above all an adventure of the mind."

Eugene Ionesco (1909 – 1994)

Chapter 1
Big Needles – The Basics

Why are those needles so big? Are they easy to use? How much do they weigh? Will my hands get tired? Do I need any special yarns? What are the possibilities? These are just some of the questions people ask when they see knitters working with Extreme Needles©, the needles designed by United Kingdom-based fiber artist Rachel John.

Working with Extreme Needles© may seem daunting at first, but once you hold them, you'll find that they are lightweight, smooth, and very easy to use. With these tips found on the following pages to get you started, you'll soon find yourself quite able to knit with ease.

Knitters will discover that projects work up extremely fast: a scarf, a simple t-shirt, or a pillow can be done in a few hours. Handbags, rugs, sweaters, or afghans can each be done in a day or two. This unique approach to knitting is easy, quick, and very satisfying – perfect for fiber artists who like immediate gratification!

The Big Needles

The needles come in a variety of lengths, ranging from short double pointed needles to straight needles at 16" (400mm), 20" (500mm), 24" (600mm), 28" (700mm), and 32" (800mm) lengths. As you knit, hold them loosely. When working with any size needle, especially the longer ones, be sure the weight of the needles (and the knitting) rests in your lap, rather than in your hands or wrists.

Comfort is Key!

Shorter needles (16" [400mm], 20" [500mm], and double pointed needles) can be used in the same way you might use a more standard size set of needles. Find a comfortable chair and get started!

Longer needles (24" [600mm], 28" [700mm], and 32" [800mm]) may require a bit of setup. For maximum comfort, try sitting in an armless chair, love seat, or comfortable couch. If your chair or sofa is deep, you may find it easier to work more towards the front edge rather than sitting back. By placing several pillows behind, you will ensure good back support, and will relieve tension and stress on the upper body.

How to Hold the Needles

When working with the needles, there are two basic techniques that make Big Stitch Knitting easy:

In Your Lap

Using your lap for support, hold the needles flat and keep your stitches close to the tips. This position focuses the weight of the yarn on your lap rather than placing stress on your arms or wrists.

Tent on the Couch

Position the needles on either side of you, with the base of the needles resting on your couch or chair. Bring the tips of the needles together to form a triangle shape. As above, keep your stitches close to the top point of the triangle, moving stitches from one needle to the other.

Controlling Your Yarns

Before you begin a project, take the time to place your yarns in containers that will help minimize tangles.

Depending on the size of the container, up to four balls should fit comfortably.

If you are using cones, in order to minimize tangles, make sure that they are close enough together that they will not fall over and roll around.

Casting On

When starting a new project, a long-tail cast on method works best, but as you become more comfortable with the needles and working with multiple fibers at the same time, try other techniques to find what works best for you.

When casting on, be sure to do so loosely. As you become acquainted with Big Stitch Knitting, you'll find the first few rows can be a little tight; casting on evenly and generously can help ease this tightness.

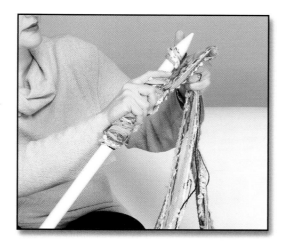

Whether you knit continental or American style, the thumb of your left hand can be very helpful in making sure that you catch all of the fibers in each stitch. Before inserting the right hand needle in each stitch, move your left thumb under the stitch. (If you knit left handed, this will be your right thumb, of course!)

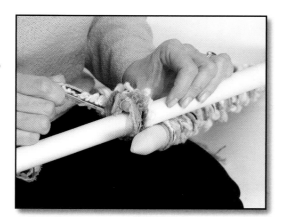

As You Are Knitting

Pull the yarns straight up out of the containers, and as you do this, watch carefully for tangles and knots. Further, be sure to keep an eye out for the end of a ball in order to anticipate adding new yarns.

Once you have completed the first row, be sure to pull the slack at the beginning of all subsequent rows to ensure even and finished-looking edges. This technique is especially useful when creating I-Cords later in the projects. As you finish each row, gently pull the knitted fabric down and spread it evenly. Be careful not to pull on the fabric too hard, as doing so may make the stitches on the needle too tight.

Knit the Twist!

A tip when using multiple fibers is that you may find the yarns will twist together. This is normal.

Even though this can be minimized by organizing your yarns carefully (see **Controlling Your Yarns**), when a twist develops, tighten the twist towards the needles and incorporate the twist into the subsequent stitches. It may take three or four stitches to incorporate the entire twist.

Worming

Occasionally, yarns will refuse to work together despite how you organize them. For example, you may find that a fiber will not pull at the same tension as the others, and as a result, it will create small loops that may not be evident at the time you create the stitch. This is known as "worming."

These annoyances can either be addressed at the end of the project or as you go, tying them off with an overhand knot as close to the stitch as you can.

Once tied, trim the loop near the knot and it will disappear into the larger stitch.

Now that we've walked through the basics, you're ready for your Big Stitch adventure!

This is a great first 'Big Stitch' project, using basic stitches and long needles.

Finished Measurements

- 46"/117cm long x 8"/20cm wide

Skill Level Beginner

Wool Weight

- Yarn Standard #5

Materials

- 3, 140g (255 yd/234m) balls **Bernat** *Soft Boucle* (97% acrylic, 3% polyester) color #26515

Tools

- Size 35 US (19mm) 20" (500mm) or 24" (600mm) straight needles
- Large eye darning needle

Gauge

- 5 sts x 8 rows = 4"/10cm in Pattern Stitch with 3 strands held tog

Designer Notes

- Scarf is worked sideways.

Pattern Stitch

Row 1 (RS): Knit.
Row 2: Purl.
Row 3: Purl.
Row 4: Knit.
Rep Rows 1-4 to form the Pattern Stitch.

Scarf

With 3 strands held together, loosely CO 80 sts.
Beg Row 1 of Pattern Stitch.
Continue even in Pattern Stitch, repeating Rows 1-4, 4 times [16 total rows].
BO all sts loosely.

Finishing

Weave in all ends.

Pockets

With RS facing, create a 9"/23cm fold at one end of scarf so that RS faces RS.
With 1 strand of yarn and darning needle, sew side seams at cast on edge and bind off edge.
Repeat for other end of scarf.

Make It Your Own!

- Add fringe to the pocket edge.
- Use a different pattern stitch.
- Add beads to the pocket edge.

Pumpkin

This easy piece is knitted from side to side and works up in no time flat for an attractive and very cuddly accessory.

Sizes

- Wrap is sized for a Women's Small/Medium and Large/X-Large.

Finished Measurements

- Back (neck to hem) 30 (34)"/ 76 (86)cm
- Length 68 (72)"/173 (183)cm

Skill Level Beginner

Wool Weight

- *Yarn Standard #6*

Materials

- 6, (140 yd/128m) hanks **Decadent Fibers** *Crème Puff* color Pumpkin

Optional colorway:
- 6, (140 yd/128m) hanks **Decadent Fibers** *Crème Puff* color Avocado Bluechip

Tools

- Size 50 US (25mm) 24" (600mm) straight needles

Gauge

- 4 sts x 8 rows = 4"/10cm in Garter st with 2 strands held tog

Designer Notes

- Wrap is worked in one piece.
- Wrap is knitted sideways beginning at Front edge, across Back, to other Front.
- Embellish with large shawl pin as closure or as decoration.

Wrap

With 2 strands held together, CO 8 (12) sts.
Inc row (RS): K1, inc 1, knit to end [1 st inc'd].
Knit 1 row.
Rep last 2 rows, 21 more times [30 (34) sts].
Work even in Garter st until piece measures 46 (50)"/117 (127)cm [24 (28) rows more] from CO, ending after a WS row.
Dec row (RS): K1, K2tog, knit to end [1 st dec'd].
Knit 1 WS row.
Repeat last two rows, 21 more times.
BO rem 8 (12) sts.

Finishing

Weave in all ends.

Make It Your Own!

- Choose 3 different colors and stripe the piece as you go.
- Choose 3 shades of the same color and merge them in a pattern.

Avocado Bluechip

Can something this beautiful really be easy?
Absolutely!

Caribbean Sea Afghan

Finished Measurements

- 50"/127cm long x 60"/152cm wide

Skill Level Easy

Wool Weight

- Yarn Standard #4

Materials

- 16, 50g (85 yd/78m) skeins **Berroco** *Cotton Twist Variegated* (70% mercerized cotton, 30% rayon) color #8460 Pool Party (MC)
- 8, 25g (95 yd/87m) skeins **Berroco** *Lumina* (54% cotton, 36% acrylic, 10% polyester) color #1610 Fairy Dust (A)
- 16, 50g (92 yd/85m) skeins **Berroco** *Foliage* (53% wool, 47% acrylic) color #5930 Russian Sage (B)
- 8, 100g (210 yd/192m) skeins **Berroco** *Comfort* (50% super fine nylon, 50% super fine acrylic) color #9753 Aegean Sea (C)

Tools

- Size 50 US (25mm) 24" (600mm) straight needles

Gauge

- 6 sts x 9 rows = 4"/10cm in Linen St holding 2 strands of MC, 1 strand of A, 2 strands of B, and 2 strands of C held tog

Linen Stitch (multiple of 2 sts)

Row 1 (RS): *K1, sl 1 pwise wyif; rep from * to end.
Row 2: *P1, sl 1 kwise wyib; rep from * to end.
Repeat Rows 1-2 for Linen St.

Afghan

With 2 strands of MC, 1 strand of A, 2 strands of B, and 2 strands of C held together, CO 72 sts.
Work Row 1 of Linen Stitch pattern.
Continue even in pattern until piece measures 50"/127cm, ending after a WS row.
BO all sts loosely.

Finishing

Weave in ends.

Make It Your Own!

- Add fringe on both ends.
- Sew a decorative medallion or crest onto the back of the afghan.
- Embroider your initials into one corner.

Front of Afghan

Back of Afghan

This piece works up very quickly and easily and can serve triple duty in your summer collection as a tank top, a shimmery cover for a bathing suit, or a kicky companion to silk pants and a camisole.

Sizes

- Top is sized to fit Women's Small (Medium, Large, X-Large).

Finished Measurements

- Chest 41½ (46½, 49½, 53)"/105 (118, 126, 135)cm
- Length 32½ (33½, 35, 35)"/82.5 (83.5, 89, 89)cm
- Upper Arm 19¼ (20, 20¾, 20¾)"/49 (50.8, 52.7, 52.7)cm

Skill Level Intermediate

Wool Weight

- Yarn Standard #4

Materials

- 6 (6, 9, 9), 100g (110 yds/3m) balls **Trendsetter** Minestrone (75% polyamide, 24% acrylic, 1% polyester) color #11

Tools

- Size 50 US (25mm) 16" (400mm) or 20" (500mm) straight needles
- 2 ring markers
- 4 split stitch markers

Gauge

- 5 sts x 10 rows = 4"/10cm in Garter st holding 3 strands tog

Back

With 3 strands held together, CO 26 (29, 31, 33) sts.
Row 1: Knit.
Work even in Garter st until piece measures 24" (61cm) from CO. Insert split stitch markers into knitted fabric at both ends to indicate placement of armholes.
Continue even in Garter st until piece measures 33½ (34, 34½, 34½)" / 85 (86.4, 87,6, 87.6)cm from CO.

Shape Shoulders and Neck

Row 1 (RS): K7 (8, 9, 10) sts, pm, *K1, P1; rep from * 5 times, K0 (1, 1, 1) sts, pm, K7 (8, 9, 10) sts.
Row 2 (WS): K7 (8, 9, 10) sts, slm, P0 (1, 1, 1) sts, *K1, P1; rep from * 5 (5, 6, 6) times, slm, K7 (8, 9, 10) sts.
Repeat Rows 1-2 until piece measures 32½ (33½, 35, 35)" / 82.6 (85, 89, 89)cm from CO, ending after working a WS row.
BO all sts loosely.

Front

Work as for Back.

Sleeve

With 3 strands of MC held tog, CO 18 (19, 20, 20) sts.
Knit 2 rows.
Inc row (RS): K1, inc 1, knit to last st, inc 1, K1 [2 sts inc'd].
Knit 1 row.
Repeat last two rows twice more [24 (25, 26, 26) sts].
Work even in Garter st until piece measures 5" / 12.7cm from CO.
BO all sts loosely.

Finishing

Join Front to Back at shoulders.
With RS of Sleeve facing RS of Back/Front, positioning bind off edge of Sleeve between split ring markers and sew in place.
Sew underarm seams. Sew side seams, leaving lower 5" edge for vent.
Weave in all loose ends.

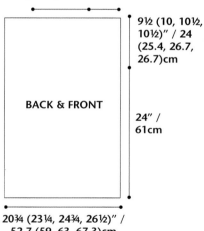

9½ (10½, 10½, 10½)" / 24 (26.7, 26.7, 26.7)cm

5½ (6½, 7, 7¾)" / 14 (16.5, 17.8, 19.7)cm

9½ (10, 10½, 10½)" / 24 (25.4, 26.7, 26.7)cm

BACK & FRONT

24" / 61cm

20¾ (23¼, 24¾, 26½)" / 52.7 (59, 63, 67.3)cm

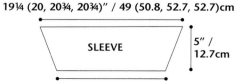

19¼ (20, 20¾, 20¾)" / 49 (50.8, 52.7, 52.7)cm

SLEEVE

5" / 12.7cm

14½ (15¼, 16, 16)" / 36.8 (38.7, 40.6, 40.6)cm

Pair this shawl with a strapless summer gown or a winter cashmere turtleneck for a perfectly accessorized evening out.

Malachite Sparkle Shawl

Finished Measurements

- 56"/142cm long x 10"/25.4cm wide (not including edging)

Skill Level Easy

Wool Weight

- *Yarn Standard #4*

Materials

- 3, (72 yd/66m) skeins **The Great Adirondack Yarn Co.** *Irise Shell* (95% rayon, 5% polyester) color Kenya II (A)
- 3, (75 yd/69m) skeins **The Great Adirondack Yarn Co.** *Ribbon Tweed* (100% rayon) color Peacock (B)
- 3, (82 yd/75m) spools **The BagSmith** *Sumptuous Silk Ribbon* (100% silk) color Jade (C)

Tools

- Size 50 (25mm) 16" (400mm) straight needles
- Size S (19mm) crochet hook

Gauge

- 8 sts x 4 rows = 4" (10cm) in pattern stitch with 1 strand of A, 1 strand of B, and 1 strand of C held tog

Linen Stitch (multiple of 2 sts)

Row 1 (RS): *K1, sl 1 pwise wyif; rep from * to end.
Row 2: *P1, sl 1 kwise wyib; rep from * to end.
Repeat Rows 1-2 for Linen St.

Shawl

With 1 strand of A, 1 strand of B, and 1 strand of C held together, CO 20 sts.
Row 1 (RS): *K1, sl 1 wyif; repeat from * to end.
Row 2: *P1, sl 1 wyib; repeat from * to end.
Repeat Rows 1-2 until piece measures 56" / 142.25cm from CO, end after working a WS row.
BO 19 sts.
Break A and B.

Crocheted Edging

With 1 strand of C and crochet hook, insert crochet hook into last st and work edging as follows:
Rnd 1: Ch 1, work 1 sc in each st around piece and join to first ch.
Rnd 2: *Work 1 slip st in each of the next 2 sc, (sl st, ch 3, 1 dc, ch 3, sl st) in next sc; rep from * to end and join to first slip st.
Fasten off.

Finishing

Weave in all ends.

Slightly oversized
and incredibly warm,
this jacket will see you
through the early winter.

Sizes

- Jacket is sized to fit Women's Small/Medium (Large/X-Large, XXX-Large).

Finished Measurements

- Chest 44 (48, 52)"/112 (122, 132)cm
- Length 31 (32, 33)"/78.8 (81.3, 83.8)cm
- Upper Arm 17¼ (17¼, 17¼)"/43.8 (43.8, 43.8)cm

Skill Level Intermediate

Wool Weight

- Yarn Standard #6 (MC)

Materials

- 20 (20, 25) 100g (109 yd/100m) balls **AslanTrends** La Pampa (55% Wool, 45% Mohair) color #45 Ceniza Grey (MC)
- 6 (6, 7) 50g (205 yd/188m) balls **Ironstone Yarns** Paris Nights (67% Acrylic, 12% Metal, 21% Nylon) color #21 Pirate (CC)
- (5) 2"/5cm round felted buttons; sample used handmade buttons by Bonnie Tuscano

Tools

- Size 35 US (19mm) 20" (500mm) straight needles
- Size 50 US (25mm) 24" (600mm) straight needles
- Size N/15 US (10mm) crochet hook
- 2 large stitch holders
- 2 large split stitch markers
- 5 small split stitch markers

Gauge

- 4 sts x 5 rows = 4"/10cm in St st, holding 5 strands of MC and 2 strands of CC tog on larger ndls
- 18 sts x 6 rows = 4"/10cm in St st, holding 3 strands of MC and 2 strands of CC tog on smaller ndls

Designer Notes

- Body is worked back and forth in one piece to underarms. Then Back and Fronts are worked separately to shoulders, using larger ndls and 5 strands of MC and 2 strands of CC held tog.
- Sleeves are worked separately, using smaller ndls and 3 strands of MC and 2 strands of CC held tog.

Body

With 5 strands of MC and 2 strands of CC held together and larger ndls, CO 45 (48, 50) sts.
Row 1 (RS): K11 (12, 13) sts, pm, K22 (24, 26) sts, pm, K11 (12, 13) sts.
Work even in Garter st for 2 rows.
Next row (WS): K2, purl to last 2 sts, K2.
Work even in St st, maintaining 2-st Garter border on both sides, until piece measures 22 (23, 24)"/56 (58.5, 61)cm from CO, ending after a WS Row.

Divide for Underarms

Next row (RS): Knit across, removing markers and placing first and last 11 (12, 13) sts on separate stitch holders for Left and Right Front.

Back

With WS facing, join 5 strands of MC and 2 strands of CC held tog.
With larger ndls, purl 1 row.
Dec row (RS): K1, SSK, knit to last 3 sts, K2tog, K1 [2 sts dec'd].
Work 1 WS row.
Rep last 2 rows, 1 more time [18 (20, 22) sts rem].

Work even in St st until piece measures 31 (32, 33)"/78.8 (81.3, 83.8)cm from CO, ending after a WS row.
BO all sts loosely.
Place split stitch markers in BO edge, 6 (6½, 7)"/15.25 (16.5, 17.8)cm from edges, to mark Shoulder placement.

Left Front

With WS facing, sl sts from stitch holder to larger ndls and join 5 strands of MC and 2 strands of CC held together.
With larger ndls, K2, purl to end.
Dec row (RS): K1, SSK, knit to end.
Work 1 WS row.
Rep last 2 rows, 1 more time [9 (10, 11) sts rem].
Work even in St st, maintaining 2-st Garter border at beg of all WS rows, until piece measures 31 (32, 33)"/78.8 (81.3, 83.8)cm from CO, ending after a WS row.
BO all sts loosely.

Right Front

With WS facing, sl sts from stitch holder to larger ndls and join 5 strands of MC and 2 strands of CC held together.
With larger ndls, purl to last 2 sts, K2.
Work as for Left Front, reversing all shaping.

Sleeves

With 3 strands of MC and 2 strands of CC held together and smaller ndls, CO 54 sts.
Row 1 (RS): *K1, P1; rep from * to last st, end K1.
Row 2: P1 *K1, P1; rep from * to end.
Rep last 2 rows until piece measures 3"/7.6cm from CO, ending after a WS row.
Inc row (RS): K1, inc 1, knit to last st, inc 1, K1 [2 sts inc'd].
Purl 1 row.
Rep these 2 rows, 11 more times [78 sts].
Work even in St st until piece measures 20"/50.8cm from CO, ending after a WS row.

Shape Sleeve Cap

At beg of next 4 rows, BO 6 sts.

Dec row (RS): K1, SSK, knit to last 3 sts, K2tog, K1.

Dec row (WS): P1, P2tog, purl to last 3 sts, P2togtbl.

Rep last 2 rows, 4 more times [34 sts rem].

BO all sts loosely.

Finishing

With RS facing, 2 strands of MC held together, and crochet hook, join Fronts to Back at shoulder seams.

Set in sleeves and sew side and underarm seams.

Collar

With RS facing, 2 strands of MC, 2 strands of CC held together, and crochet hook, work 1 sc in 14 (16, 18, 20) sts around Neck edge.

Row 2 (RS): *ch3, sk 1, sc; rep from * to end.

Row 3: *ch3, sc into ch-3 space; rep from * to end.

Fasten off.

Weave in ends.

Buttons

Sew buttons to Right Front, evenly spaced between collar edge and hem.

With split stitch markers, indicate placement of 5 buttonholes opposite buttons.

With 1 strand of MC and crochet hook, work 1 rnd sc into each marked stitch, to make and reinforce buttonhole.

Weave in all ends.

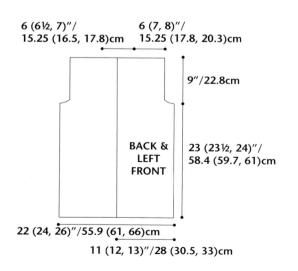

6 (6½, 7)"/ 15.25 (16.5, 17.8)cm

6 (7, 8)"/ 15.25 (17.8, 20.3)cm

9"/22.8cm

BACK & LEFT FRONT

23 (23½, 24)"/ 58.4 (59.7, 61)cm

22 (24, 26)"/55.9 (61, 66)cm

11 (12, 13)"/28 (30.5, 33)cm

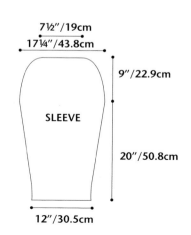

7½"/19cm

17¼"/43.8cm

9"/22.9cm

SLEEVE

20"/50.8cm

12"/30.5cm

Back

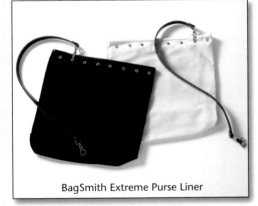

BagSmith Extreme Purse Liner

Finished Measurements

- 15"/38cm tall x 14"/35.6cm wide x 2"/5cm deep

Skill Level Easy

Wool Weight

- Yarn Standard #4

Materials

- 3, 100g (400 yd/366m) hanks **Oasis** *Aussi Sock* (90% merino, 10% nylon) color #WS03 Amethyst (A)
- 2, 100g (128 yd/117m) hanks **Oasis** *Aussi Wool* (100% wool) color #W05 Tiger Lily (B)
- 4, (187 yd/171m) hanks **The Great Adirondack Yarn Co.** *Cyclone* (100% rayon) color Eggplant Eddie (C)
- 2, (74 yd/68m) hanks **The Great Adirondack Yarn Co.** *Bali #4* (57% rayon, 33% polyester, 10% PVC) color Amethyst (D)
- 11 glass beads
- Beading thread to attach beads to bag
- 12" of nylon cord (for closure)
- **The BagSmith** *Extreme Purse Liner* Item #6050
- 1 set, **The BagSmith** *Clip Straps* Item #1451

Tools

- Size 50 US (25mm) 16" (400mm) or 20" (500mm) straight needles
- Size 50 US (25mm) double pointed needles
- Size 35 (19mm) 16" (400mm) or 20" (500mm) straight needles
- Size 10.5 (6.5mm) straight needles
- Size I/9 (5.5mm) crochet hook
- Yarn needle

Gauge

- 6 sts x 10 rows = 4"/10cm in St st with 3 strands (A), 2 strands (B), and 2 strands (C) held tog on larger ndls

Handbag Body

With 3 strands (A), 2 strands (B), and 2 strands (C) held together and larger straight ndls, CO 21 sts.
Work 4 rows in Garter st.
Next row (WS): Purl.
Continue even in St st until piece measures 14½"/36.8cm from CO, ending after a RS row.
Work 3 rows in Garter st.
Next row (RS): Cont in St st, work even until piece measures 29½"/75cm from CO, ending after a RS row.
Work 3 rows in Garter st.
BO all sts.

Handbag Collar

With 3 strands (A), 2 strands (C), and 1 strand (D) held together and smaller ndls, CO 6 sts.
Row 1 (RS): K3, yo, K3.
Row 2, 4, 6: Knit.
Row 3: K3, yo, K4.
Row 5: K3, yo, K5.
Row 7: K3, yo, K6.
Row 8: BO 4 sts, K6.
Rep Rows 1-8 five more times.
BO all sts.
With yarn needle, join cast on and bind off ends of Collar together.

Handbag Inner Facing

With 1 strand of B and Size 10.5 US (6.5mm) ndls, CO 12 sts.
Work even in Garter st until piece measures 24"/61cm from CO.
BO all sts.

With yarn needle, join cast on and bind off ends of facing together.

Finishing

Using darning needle, sew sides of Handbag together. Place *Extreme Purse Liner* inside of bag and attach to WS Handbag body with 1 strand (B) and yarn needle. Sew Collar to outside top edge of bag with 1 strand (B). Position Inner Facing inside Handbag, with WS against *Extreme Purse Liner*. Sew Inner Facing to Collar, covering top edge of *Purse Liner*.

Closure
With crochet hook and nylon cord make chain stitch loop large enough to accommodate beads for closure. Attach loop to one side of inside wall. String beads on beading thread and attach to opposite wall.

I-Cord Covers for Straps (make 2)
With 3 strands (A), 1 strand (C), and 2 strands (D) held together, CO 4 sts onto dpns, leaving a 12"/30.5cm tail.
Next row: *K4, slide sts to opposite end of ndl without turning, and pull working yarn downwards; rep from * until piece measures 24"/61cm from CO.
BO all sts, leaving a 12"/30.5cm tail.
Thread clip straps through inside of I-Cord.
Wind and fasten tails to end of straps (where they attach to the leather).
Clip straps to bag.
Weave in all ends.

Back

A lovely
complement to
summer outfits.

Finished Measurements

- 15"/38cm tall x 12"/30.5cm wide x 3"/7.6cm deep

Skill Level Intermediate

Wool Weight

- Yarn Standard #4

Materials

- 3, 9 oz (120 yd/110m) hanks **The BagSmith** *Nubbie Cotton* (100% cotton) color Natural (MC)
- 2, 4 oz (120 yd/110m) hanks **The BagSmith** *Smooth Cotton* (100% cotton) color Natural (CC)
- 1, **The BagSmith** *Extreme Purse Liner*, Item# 6051W
- 1, **Muench Yarns** 4"/10cm Grayson Leather Flower
- 1, 8"/20.3cm length of nylon cord (to attach the flower)

Tools

- Size 50 US (25mm) 16" (400mm) straight needles
- Size U US (25mm) crochet hook
- Darning needle

Gauge

- 4 sts x 8 rows = 4"/10cm in Basket Weave stitch pattern, holding 3 strands of MC and 2 strands of CC tog

Basket Weave Stitch (mult of 15 sts)

Row 1 (RS): P5, K5, P5.
Row 2: K5, P5, K5.
Row 3: Rep Row 1.
Row 4: Rep Row 2.
Row 5: Rep Row 2.
Row 6: Rep Row 1.
Row 7: Rep Row 2.
Row 8: Rep Row 1.
Rep Rows 1-8 for Pattern St.

Handbag

Back

With 3 strands of MC and 2 strands of CC held tog, CO 15 sts.
Row 1 (RS): Work Row 1 of Pattern St. Continue in pattern, working Rows 1-8 of Pattern St, rep pattern twice through [16 rows total].
Work Rows 1-4 once more.

Base

Work 4 rows Garter st.

Front

Next row (RS): Work Row 1 of Pattern St. Continue in pattern, working Rows 1-8 of Pattern St, rep pattern twice through [16 rows total].
Work Rows 1-4 of Pattern St once more.

Begin Flap

Work Rows 5-8 of Pattern St.
Beg Garter St.
Dec row (RS): K1, SSK, knit to last 3 sts, K2tog, K1 [2 sts dec'd].
Next row (WS): Knit.
Rep last two rows, three more times [4 sts rem].
With crochet hook, BO all sts as foll: insert hook into first st and ch 1, *insert hook into next st and ch 1, yarnover and pull through both loops; rep from * to end. Fasten off.

Finishing

Shoulder Strap

With 3 strands of MC and 2 strands of CC and crochet hook, work a 54"/137cm chain. Fasten off.

Assembly

Fold bag in half at garter ridges, so that CO edge meets beg of Flap shaping. With 1 strand of CC and darning ndl, whipstitch strap to sides and bottom of bag, being sure that strap is not twisted. Join end of strap to beg, leaving a shoulder strap of approx 36"/91.5cm in length.

Button Loop

With 3 strands of MC and 2 strands of CC held tog and crochet hook, ch 9 into BO edge of flap. Fasten off into first Ch and attach end securely under flap.

Attach Flower

With RS facing, attach flower to middle front of bag, approx 2"/5cm from CO edge of bag using nylon cord.

Insert Liner

Place zippered lining inside of bag and secure with darning ndl and 1 strand of CC. Weave in all ends.

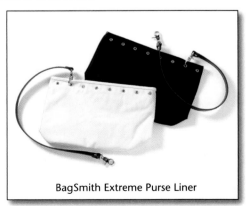

BagSmith Extreme Purse Liner

This shawl works
up fast – just a few
hours with great yarns
on the big needles.

Finished Measurements

- 60"/152.5cm long x 22"/55.9cm wide

Skill Level Easy

Wool Weight

- *Yarn Standard #5*

Materials

- 8, (75 yd/66m) skeins **The Great Adirondack Yarn Co.** *Plush* (60% rayon, 40% nylon) color Eggplant Eddie (MC)
- 1, (82 yd/75m) spool **The BagSmith** *Sumptuous Silk Ribbon* (100% silk) color Amethyst (CC)

Tools

- Size 50 US (25mm) 20" (500mm) straight needles OR SIZE TO OBTAIN GAUGE
- Size N/15 US (10mm) crochet hook
- Yarn needle

Gauge

- 6 sts x 4 rows = 4"/10cm in pattern st, with 2 strands of MC held tog

Diamond Lace Stitch (multiple of 3 sts)

Row 1 (RS): K2, *yo, K3, pass first st over second and third sts; rep from * to last st, end K1.
Row 2: Purl.
Row 3: K1, *K3, pass first st over second and third sts, yo; rep from * to last 2 sts, end K2.
Row 4: Purl.
Rep Rows 1-4 for Diamond Lace St.

Shawl

With 2 strands of MC held together, CO 30 sts.
Purl 1 row (WS).
Work Row 1 of Diamond Lace St.
Continue even in pattern as written, rep Rows 1-4 until piece measures 60"/152.4cm from CO, ending after a WS row.
BO all sts loosely.

Finishing

Weave in ends.

Fringe
With CC, cut (120) 14"/35.6cm lengths of Fringe.
Beg at CO edge, with crochet hook, loop 2 lengths of ribbon over the hook, making sure tails are even, and pull loop though edge of wrap.
Insert ends of fringe through loop and pull tightly.
Continue working across CO edge, attaching fringe evenly and generously across edge.
Attach fringe in the same manner across the BO edge.

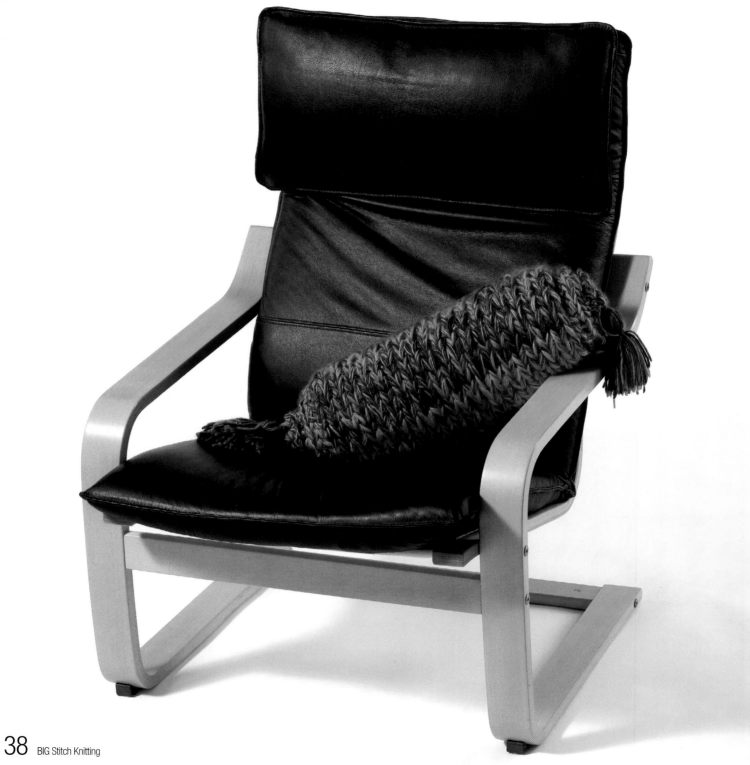

Finished Measurements

- 16"/40.6cm long (not including tassels) x 7"/17.8cm diameter

Skill Level Easy

Wool Weight

- Yarn Standard #4

Materials

- 10, 50g (100 yd/92m) balls **Trendsetter Yarns** *Tonalita* (52% Wool, 48% Acrylic) color #2348 Sunset (MC)
- (1) 15"/38cm x 6"/15.25cm tube or neck-shaped white pillow form (can be found in bedding department stores)

Tools

- Size 35 US (19mm) 20" (500mm) straight needles
- Size 35 US (19mm) double pointed needles
- Large eye darning needle

Gauge

- 5 sts x 5 rows = 4"/10cm in St st, holding 10 strands of MC together

Pillow

With 10 strands MC held together and straight needles, CO 21 sts.
Row 1 (RS): Knit.
Row 2 (WS): Purl.
Continue even in St st, rep Rows 1-2, until piece measures 22"/55.9cm from CO, ending after a WS row.
BO all sts loosely.

Finishing

Fold knitted fabric in half lengthwise. With RS facing, sew CO edge to BO edge.
Weave in ends.
Turn knitted fabric inside out and place pillow form inside fabric tube.

Make I-Cord Edges (make 2)
With 10 strands of MC held together, CO 4 sts onto dpns.
Row 1: *K3, slide sts to RH side of ndl without turning, and pulling working yarn downwards; rep from *, until I-Cord measures 19"/48.25cm from CO.
BO all sts, leaving a 10"/25.4cm tail.

Attach I-Cord
With 1 strand of MC and darning needle, whipstitch I-Cord around end of pillow, sewing I-Cord first to knitted fabric, then to itself as you coil it around in a smaller and smaller circle (see photo). Tuck end of I-Cord into center of circle and fasten off. Repeat for other end of pillow.
Weave in ends.

Tassels
Cut approximately (80) 10½"/26.7cm lengths MC for fringe.
Fold lengths of fringe in half and with 1 strand of MC and darning needle, wrap tassel approximately 1"/2.5cm from top edge.
Secure ends of wrapped yarn.
Attach tassel to center of I-Cord coils on each end of the pillow.

Create Your Own Pillow Pattern!

There are many sizes and shapes of pillow forms available on the market. You might also have an old pillow that can use a new color or look. Creating your own cover is fun and easy.

Pick out your yarns and stitch pattern. Check your gauge by working a swatch in the stitch pattern you've chosen, and at least 10 sts on Size 35 US (19mm) needles. You will need both the number of sts per inch and the number of rows per inch.

Calculate the number of *stitches* you will need by multiplying the number of sts per inch by the width of the pillow.
Calculate the number of *rows* you will need by multiplying the number of rows per inch by the height of the pillow.

If the pillow has a gusset, decide if you will knit a separate piece to go around the gusset or include extra stitches in the body pattern.

You can make the pillow cover in one piece and sew up the sides, or make several pieces that are sewn or crocheted together.

Here is an example
of using Big Stitch
embellishments with
smaller stitch projects.

Skirt

Designer Notes

- Skirt is worked in one piece in the round, from hem edge to waistband.

Skirt

CO 140 (152, 160, 168) sts.
Place marker and join for working in the round, being careful not to twist sts.
Rnd 1: Knit.
Rnd 2: Purl.
Rep Rnds 1-2 once more.
Rnd 5: Knit.
Work even in St st until piece measures 13 (13½, 14, 14½)"/33 (34.3, 35.6, 36.8)cm from CO.
Next rnd: 18 (19, 20, 21) sts, pm, 18 (19, 20, 21) sts, pm, K17 (19, 20, 21) sts, pm, K17 (19, 20, 21) sts, pm, K18 (19, 20, 21) sts, pm, K18 (19, 20, 21) sts, pm, K18 (19, 20, 21) sts, pm, K18 (19, 20, 21) sts.
Dec rnd: Knit to first m, K2tog, *knit to next m, K2tog; rep from * around [132 (144, 152, 160) sts rem].
Next rnd: Knit, removing all markers.
Work even in St st until piece measures 15½ (16, 16½, 17)"/39.4 (40.6, 41.9, 43.2)cm from CO.
BO all sts loosely.

Finishing

Pin waistband to top of skirt on WS, approx 1"/2.5cm from BO edge.
Fold BO edge over waistband and with yarn and yarn needle, sew waistband in place, being careful not to sew too tightly or twist the waistband.
Weave in all ends.

Sarong Sizes

- Sarong is sized for S/M and L/XL with drawstring waistband. This piece should be full with loose folds.

Finished Measurements

- Waist 31 (36)"/78.7 (91.4)cm
- Length 16 (17)" /40.6 (43.2)cm

Skill Level Intermediate

Wool Weight

- Yarn Standard #6

Materials

- 2 (2), (80 yd/74m) skeins **Pagewood Farm** Mohair Locks (100% wool) color Natural Greys and Blacks

Tools

- Size 50 US (25mm) 20" (500mm) straight needles
- Size 35 US (19mm) double pointed needles
- Large eye darning needle

Gauge

- 6 sts x 8 rows = 4"/10cm in Garter St on larger ndls

Designer Notes

- To wear sarong, place drawstring at waist length, distribute sarong fabric across waist and hips evenly. Tie drawstring in a bow.

Sarong

With Size 50 US (25mm) needles and 1 strand of *Mohair Locks,* CO 65 (70) sts.
Row 1 (RS): Knit.
Work even in Garter st until piece measures 16 (17)"/40.6 (43.2)cm from CO.
BO all sts.

Finishing

I-Cord Drawstring
With Size 35 US (19mm) dpns and 1 strand of *Mohair Locks,* CO 3 sts.
Row 1: *K3, slide sts to RH side of ndl without turning, and pulling working yarn downwards; rep from *, until I-Cord meas 54 (58)"/137.2 (147.3)cm.
BO all sts leaving a 10"/25.4cm tail.

Install Drawstring
With I-Cord tail threaded into large eye darning needle, weave I-Cord in and out of every third st across BO edge of Sarong.
Weave in all ends.

Sarong

Vest
Back

With Size 10 US (6mm) needles and MC, CO 82 (90, 100, 108) sts. Knit 1 row. Work even in Garter st until piece measures 1¼ (1½, 1½, 1½)"/3.2 (3.8, 3.8, 3.8)cm from CO. **Next row (WS):** Purl. Work even in St st until piece measures 9½ (9¾, 9¾, 9¾)"/24.1 (24.8, 24.8, 24.8)cm from CO, end after a WS row.

Shape Armholes
At beg of next 2 rows, BO 6 (6, 7, 8) sts and work to end in patt. **Next row (RS):** K1, SSK, knit to last 3 sts, K2tog, K1 [2 sts dec'd]. Purl 1 row. Rep last 2 rows 6 (9, 10, 11) more times [56 (58, 64, 68) sts rem]. Work even in St st until piece measures 19 (19¾, 20½, 20¾)"/48.3 (50.2, 52.1, 52.7)cm from CO, end after a WS row.

Shape, Back Neck and Shoulders
K17 (17, 19, 20) sts, join new ball of yarn and BO 22 (24, 26, 28), K17 (17, 19, 20) sts.
Left Shoulder
Row 1 (WS): Purl 1 row. **Row 2:** Knit. **Row 3 (WS):** BO 7 (7, 8, 8) sts and purl to end. **Row 4:** Knit.
Row 5: BO 8 sts and purl to end. BO rem 2 (2, 3, 4) sts.
Right Shoulder
Work as for Left Shoulder, reversing all shaping.

Vest Sizes

- Vest is sized to fit Women's Small (Medium, Large, X-Large).

Finished Measurements

- Chest 40 (44, 48, 53)"/101.6 (111.8, 121.9, 134.6)cm
- Length 20 (20¾, 21½, 21¾)"/ 50.8 (52.7, 54.6, 55.3)cm

Skill Level Intermediate

Wool Weight

- Yarn Standard #4 & #6

Materials

- 1 (1, 2, 3), (250 yd/229m) skeins **Pagewood Farm** *Superwash Merino* (100% Merino wool) Color Natural Black (MC)
- 1, (80 yd/74m) skein **Pagewood Farm** *Mohair Locks* (100% wool) Color Natural Greys and Black (CC)

Tools

- Size 10 US (6mm) straight needles
- Size 17 US (12mm) straight needles
- Size 35 (19mm) 16" (400mm) straight needles
- Size J US (6mm) crochet hook
- Size S US (19mm) crochet hook
- Sewing pins, darning needle

Gauge

- 18 sts x 24 rows = 4"/10cm in St st with 1 strand of MC on Size 10 US (6mm) ndls

Right Front

With Size 10 US (6mm) needles and MC, CO 41 (45, 50, 54) sts. Knit 1 row. Work even in Garter st until piece measures 1¼ (1½, 1½, 1½)"/3.2 (3.8, 3.8, 3.8)cm from CO. **Next row (WS):** Purl. Work even in St st until piece measures 9½ (9¾, 9¾, 9¾)"/24.1 (24.8, 24.8, 24.8)cm from CO, end after a RS row.

Shape Neck and Armhole

At beg of next row, BO 6 (6, 7, 8) sts and purl to end.
Row 1 (RS): K1, SSK, knit to last 3 sts, K2tog, K1.
Row 2: Purl. **Row 3:** Knit to last 3 sts, K2tog, K1.
Row 4: Purl. Rep Rows 1-4, 2 (3, 4, 4) more times.
Sizes Medium and X-Large Only
Rep Rows 1 and 2, once more.
All Sizes
Dec row (RS): K1, SSK, knit to end. Work 3 rows even in St st. Rep last 4 rows, 7 (6, 7, 7) more times [17 (17, 19, 20) sts rem]. Work even in St st until piece measures 19 (19¾, 20½, 20¾)"/48.3 (50.2, 52.1, 52.7)cm from CO, end after a RS row.

Shape Shoulders

Row 1 (WS): Purl 1 row. **Row 2:** Knit. **Row 3 (WS):** BO 7 (7, 8, 8) sts and purl to end.
Row 4: Knit. **Row 5:** BO 8 sts and purl to end. BO rem 2 (2, 3, 4) sts.

Left Front

Work as for Right Front, reversing all shaping.

Collar

With Size US 17 (12mm) needles and CC, CO 40 (42, 44, 46) sts. Knit 3 rows. Change to US 35 needles (19mm) and knit 3 rows. BO all sts.
Optional Bind-Off: For a more generous edge, BO with larger crochet hook as foll: insert hook into first st and ch 1, *insert hook into next st and ch 1, yarnover and pull through both loops; rep from * to end. Fasten off.

Finishing

Sew shoulder and side seams. Weave in all ends.

Armhole Edging

With smaller crochet hook and MC, beginning at side seam, work 1 row sc around armholes.

Front Edging

With smaller crochet hook and MC, work 1 row sc on Front edge from neck shaping to hem.

Install Collar

Pin collar to neckline and sew or crochet in place.
Optional: For a larger collar, work several rows of sc across outer edge of collar, using larger hook and CC.

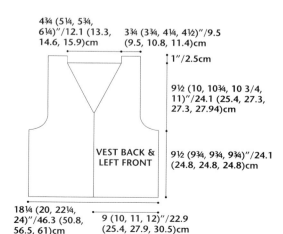

4¾ (5¼, 5¾, 6¼)"/12.1 (13.3, 14.6, 15.9)cm

3¾ (3¾, 4¼, 4½)"/9.5 (9.5, 10.8, 11.4)cm

1"/2.5cm

9½ (10, 10¾, 10 3/4, 11)"/24.1 (25.4, 27.3, 27.3, 27.94)cm

VEST BACK & LEFT FRONT

9½ (9¾, 9¾, 9¾)"/24.1 (24.8, 24.8, 24.8)cm

18¼ (20, 22¼, 24)"/46.3 (50.8, 56.5, 61)cm

9 (10, 11, 12)"/22.9 (25.4, 27.9, 30.5)cm

"I didn't play at collecting. No cigar anywhere was safe from me."

Edward G. Robinson (1893 – 1973)

Chapter 2
Working with Your Stash

Anyone who has been knitting for a while has a stash of yarns made up of odds and ends from previous projects and full balls or skeins of yarns that they just couldn't pass up at their favorite yarn shops. I know many knitters who buy yarn while traveling, not knowing what they will use it for later. One of my favorite knitting friends keeps all remnants 12"/30.5cm or longer for future use.

While many of the patterns in this book are written with specific yarns in mind, other patterns are designed for you to choose your own yarns. These patterns offer a great opportunity to use yarns from your stash, or combinations of yarns you have always wanted to work with from your Local Yarn Shop (LYS).

I can't pass up a yarn shop. The fibers call to me, and many are added to my stash. I have bags of yarns I purchased from my LYS, Fine Points in Cleveland, Ohio, where the owner, Liz Tekus, lovingly assembles great combinations of yarns in sale packs. The assortments are usually in the same color family with varying textures and weights of yarns.

Fiber Selection

Suppose you want to knit an afghan with yarns from your stash using a range of fibers across different weights and textures. Begin by organizing and choosing your yarns according to color. When making your selections, avoid those that will not play well on the big needles, such as chenille and acrylic mohair (real mohair will work fine). Try to combine yarns that will minimize the amount of tangling and worming.

Your selection of yarns should include 7-12 strands to work on the Size 50 US (25mm) needles. The resulting "big yarn" will give you a nice weight. Place each ball or skein into containers. This will assist you in preventing the yarns from tangling as you knit. Three to four balls should fit in each container — as long as they will not "stick" to each other ("sticky" yarns should be placed in their own containers to prevent tangling).

Swatch It

Now is the time to check the compatibility of your yarns by knitting a swatch. Cast on twelve stitches, holding all the strands together. Work even in Stockinette Stitch (knit 1 row, purl 1 row) for six rows. Bind off all stitches. Once the swatch is complete, you should be able to see if any of the yarns don't work well together — either in terms of color or texture.

Stitch Gauge and Density

"If you don't know where you are going, any road will get you there."
Lewis Carroll (1832 – 1898)

When considering gauge and big needles, it is a general rule of thumb that you will get approximately 1 stitch per inch (2.5cm) on the Size 50 US (25mm) needles and 5 stitches over 4"/10cm using Size 35 US (19mm) needles, when using a combination of conventional yarns.

The greater the number of yarns you use (and the larger the fibers), the denser and thicker the stitch. You may end up with a smaller or larger gauge depending on the combinations of yarns you choose. If you want to make sure your gauge is accurate for a pattern, increase or decrease the number of fibers in your swatch until you have the exact gauge. Make up swatches of 10 sts x 10 rows so that you can evaluate the stitch count.

When working with roving, the stitches can become quite dense and the gauge may increase, depending on the thickness of the prepared roving. You can prepare the roving by dividing it in half or in quarters. Be careful to pull it apart evenly to ensure a consistent gauge. Thinner roving results in more stitches per inch. Conversely, the thicker the roving, the fewer stitches you will have in your gauge.

Stitch Gauge and Density Tips

- You may use similar weight yarns or combine a variety of weights as you work on projects. The swatch (see **Swatch It** above) plays a vital role in showing how colors and weights will work together.
- To maintain a consistent gauge, be sure that when you run out of a fiber, replace it with another that is similar in weight.
- To join two ends (new yarn to working yarn), use an overhand knot to tie the ends together, leaving a short tail. When using a great number of fibers, knots disappear easily into the knitted fabric and tails can be easily trimmed.
- With fewer fibers, crocheting or weaving in ends will create a more finished piece.

Here are a few examples of projects in this book that use different combinations of strand count and yarn weights:

- *The Cuddle* (page 20) uses two strands of super bulky yarn on Size 50 US (25mm) needles.

- *The Stashionista Throw* (page 64) uses a combination of 14 yarns on Size 50 US (25mm) needles, including several fingering weight and bulky yarns — and a few in between. This project also includes a "carry along" metallic yarn that does not affect the gauge or density of the stitch at all, but it adds a little sparkle to the piece.

- The *Simple Pocket Scarf* (page 18) uses 3 strands of the same yarn on Size 35 US (19mm) needles.

- The *Elegant Carpet Bag* (page 86) uses a quarter piece of roving on Size 35 US (19mm) needles.

The Cuddle
(page 20)

The Stashionista Throw
(page 64)

The *Simple Pocket Scarf*
(page 18)

The *Elegant Carpet Bag*
(page 86)

Combining Textured Fibers

Below, you'll find examples of five scarves made using Seed Stitch, Size 50 US (25mm) needles, and a combination of five yarns: four from The Great Adirondack Yarn Company (color Grapevine), and *Sumptuous Silk Ribbon* from The BagSmith (color Sapphire). In each scarf, the overall appearance changes depending on the number of strands and textures of the yarns.

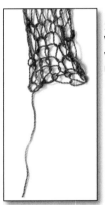

Single Strand Scarf
Wool Crepe (70% wool, 18% nylon, 3% metallic)

Two Strand Scarf
Wool Crepe and Cyclone (100% rayon)

Three Strand Scarf
Wool Crepe, Cyclone, and Rayon Loop (100% rayon)

Four Strand Scarf
Wool Crepe, Cyclone, Rayon Loop, and Silk Ribbon (100% silk)

Five Strand Scarf
Wool Crepe, Cyclone, Rayon Loop, Silk Ribbon, and New Persian (100% nylon)

Working with Color – Improvise!

"Life is a lot like jazz...it's best when you improvise..."
George Gershwin (1898 – 1937)

In music, if you heard the same note played over and over, it'd be more than just boring, it'd be annoying! But, when you combine that one note with others and add different instruments, you experience a variety of interesting sounds and textures.

Music can create extreme moods and experiences; the same is true when working with color. No one color is important just in itself. In paintings, each color is seen as part of a dynamic interaction with other colors. Any arrangement can evoke sensations of pleasure or discomfort depending on their presentation.

To develop your color "eye," study the wonderfully inexhaustible supply of exciting combinations in nature ranging from the wildly extravagant (such as peacock feathers) to the soft and muted (as in rocks and shells). Experiment with turning these "color schemes" into combinations of fibers. Remember that there are no exact rules for creating pleasing effects in color relationships, only possibilities — so IMPROVISE!

"Life is a big canvas, and you should throw all the paint you can on it."
Danny Kaye (1913 – 1987)

The Color Wheel

Looking at the color wheel, the safest combinations are those that are close to each other, making them good places to start experimenting.

High contrast colors will pop against each other: yellow against blue, red versus green.

To find other combinations like these, look at the complementary colors opposite one another on the color wheel.

When working with monochromatic fibers, try adding a little contrast by adding an additional color or one with a bit of metallic.

Cool combinations are calming
and soothing.

Warm and hot combinations are
energetic, exciting, and fiery.

Warm and cool together present
opportunities for contrast.

Earth tones such as beige, browns,
and copper are grounding.

Stitch Patterns

"Creativity can be described as letting go of certainties."
Gail Sheehy (1937 –)

Stitch patterns appear differently when using big needles. Subtle details found in knitted fabric made on smaller needles can be much more evident when worked on larger needles, especially when using multiple strands of the same yarn. Multiples of different types of fibers present a more textured look.

When first working with the needles, the best stitches to start with are those that require the least amount of wrist action. Once you've achieved a greater comfort level with the needles, experiment with more complex stitch patterns or create your own.

These are but a few stitch patterns that will get your creative juices flowing!

Garter Stitch

Garter Stitch (any number of sts)
Row 1: Knit.
Rep Row 1 for pattern stitch.

The Cuddle (page 20)

Seed Stitch

Seed Stitch (multiple of 2 sts + 1)
Row 1: *K1, P1*; rep from * to last st, K1.
Row 2: *P1, K1; rep from * to last st, P1.
Repeat Rows 1-2 for pattern stitch.

Stashionista Wall Hanging (page 62)

Stockinette Stitch

Stockinette Stitch (any number of sts)
Row 1: Knit.
Row 2: Purl.
Repeat Rows 1-2 for pattern stitch.

Wrapped Roving Rug (page 88)

Linen Stitch

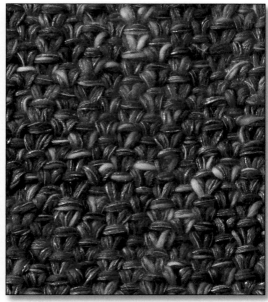

Linen Stitch (even number of sts)
Row 1: *K1, sl 1 pwise wyib; rep from * to end.
Row 2: *P1, sl 1 kwise wyif.
Rep Rows 1-2 for pattern stitch.

Caribbean Sea Afghan (page 22)

The colors of autumn combine with cozy, luscious fibers to keep the fall winds at bay.

Finished Measurements

- Length 44"/112cm
- Width (at widest point) 12"/30.5cm
- Width (at narrowest point) 4"/10cm

Skill Level Easy

Wool Weight

- *Yarn Standard #3 & #4*

Materials

- 120 yds/110m each of 3 DK weight yarns (Yarn Standard #3)
- 120 yds/110m each of 2 worsted weight yarns (Yarn Standard #4)

Tools

- Size 35 US (19mm) 20" (500mm) straight needles
- Large eye darning needle

Gauge

- 5 sts x 6 rows = 4"/10cm in Pattern Stitch with 5 strands held tog

Pattern Stitch

Row 1 (RS): K1, *yo, K2, pass yo over 2 sts; rep from * to last st, K1.
Row 2: Purl.
Row 3: K1, *K2, pass the first st over the second, yo; rep from * to last st, K1.
Row 4: Purl.
Rep Rows 1-4 for Pattern St.

Ascot

With 5 strands held together, CO 20 sts.
Work 2 rows in Garter St.
Next row (RS): Work Row 1 of Pattern St, rep pattern 9 times across row.
Cont in pattern until piece measures 11"/28cm from CO, end after a WS row.
Dec row (RS): *K2tog, rep from * to end [10 sts rem].
Purl 1 row.
Work even in Pattern St until piece measures 33"/84cm from CO, end after a WS row.
Inc row (RS): *Kfb; rep from * to end [20 sts].
Purl 1 row.
Next row (RS): Work Row 1 of Pattern St, rep pattern 9 times across row.
Cont in pattern until piece measures 43½"/111cm from CO, end after a WS row.
Work 2 rows in Garter St.
BO all sts loosely.

Finishing

Weave in ends.

A fresh, bright
look for early spring.

Scarf of Spring Greens

Pattern Stitch (multiple of 3 sts)

Row 1 (WS): Purl.
Row 2: K2, *yo, K3, pass 1st of 3 knit sts over 2nd and 3rd sts; rep from * to last st, end K1.
Row 3: Purl.
Row 4: K1, *K3, pass 1st of 3 knit sts over 2nd and 3rd sts, yo; rep from * to last 2 sts, end K2.
Rep Rows 1-4 for Pattern St.

Scarf

With 7 strands held together, CO 9 sts.
Work Row 1 of Pattern St.
Continue even in pattern until piece measures 54"/137cm from CO, ending after working Row 1 of Pattern St.
BO all sts loosely.

Finishing

Scarf Edging
With crochet hook and 7 strands, work 1 sc in every stitch and row around scarf.
Fasten off.
Weave in all ends.

Finished Measurements

- 13"/33cm long x 13"/33cm wide, not including fringe

Skill Level Beginner

Wool Weight

- *Yarn Standard #2, #3, #4 & #5*

Materials

- 120 yds/110m each of 2 sport weight yarns (Yarn Standard #2)
- 120 yds/110m each of 1 DK weight (Yarn Standard #3)
- 120 yds/110m each of 1 worsted weight (Yarn Standard #4)
- 120 yds/110m each of 5 bulky weights (Yarn Standard #5)
- (1) 12"/30.5cm-square white polyester-filled pillow (can be found at most craft stores)
- Several yards of smooth yarn in a complementary color (to sew seams)

Tools

- Size 50 US (25mm) 16" (400mm) straight needles
- Size N/15 US (10mm) crochet hook
- Sewing pins
- Large eye darning needle

Gauge

- 4 sts x 5 rows = 4"/10cm in Stockinette St

Pillow

With 9 yarns held together, CO 16 sts.
Row 1 (RS): Knit.
Row 2: Purl.
Rep Row 1-2, working even in St st until piece measures 12"/30.5cm from CO, ending after a WS row.
Work 2 rows in Garter st.
Next row (RS): Knit.
Work even in St st until piece measures 26"/66cm from CO, ending after a WS row.
BO all sts loosely.

Finishing

With WS of knitted fabric facing the pillow form, pin cover in place. With darning needle and a smooth yarn in a complementary color, sew side and bottom seams around pillow form, removing pins as seams are complete. Weave in ends.

Fringe

With yarns used for pillow, cut fringe into 8"/20.3cm lengths. Insert crochet hook through both Front and Back layers of fabric. With one or more strands of fringe, drape strand(s) evenly in notch of hook and pull loop through, then insert the tails through the loop and pull tightly. Continue around, placing the strand(s) as desired.

Pillow without the fringe

This project is an easy
and fun way to add color
to a special room. You can
easily make one to fit your
décor and space needs.
Begin by raiding your stash!

Finished Measurements

- 39"/99cm long x 22"/56cm wide

Skill Level Easy

Wool Weight

- *Yarn Standard #3, #4 & #5*

Materials

- 60 yds/55m of 12 DK weight or larger yarns, color group Purple (A)
- 60 yds/55m of 12 DK weight or larger yarns, color group Dark Blue (B)
- 60 yds/55m of 12 DK weight or larger yarns, color group Medium Blue (C)
- 60 yds/55m of 12 DK weight or larger yarns, color group Light Blue (D)
- 60 yds/55m of 12 DK weight or larger yarns, color group Aqua (E)
- (1) 32"/81.3cm curtain rod, flag pole, dowel rod, or appropriate hardware to hang the piece

Tools

- Size 35 US (19mm) 24" (600mm) straight needles
- Large eye darning needle

Gauge

- 5 sts x 7 rows = 4"/10cm in Seed St with 12 strands held tog

Designer Notes

- Vary the yarn weights over DK, worsted, and bulky within color groups.
- Once hung, piece may stretch depending on length, yarns used, and density of stitches. The denser the knitted fabric, the less significantly it will stretch.

Seed Stitch (odd number of stitches)

Row 1 (RS): *K1, P1; rep from * to last st, K1.
Repeat Row 1 for Seed St.

Wall Hanging

With 12 strands from darkest color group (A) held together, CO 25 sts.
Work Row 1 of Seed St.
Continue in Seed St until piece measures approximately 6"/15.25cm.
Continue in Seed St as established, and begin next color group (B) by replacing 2 yarns every row over the next 6 rows with 2 new (B) yarns. When all strands from (A) have been exchanged for new color group (B), work even in Seed St and color group (B) for approximately 3"/7.6cm.
Rep from * to * until all groups have been incorporated.

Rod Pocket
Work even in Seed St for an additional 3"/7.6cm.
BO all sts.

Finishing

Fold bind off edge over to WS, creating a 3"/7.6cm rod pocket. With darning needle and a worsted weight yarn from color group E, sew bind off edge to WS, leaving side edges open. Weave in all ends. Slip pole through pocket and attach to wall.

Finished Measurements

- 59"/150cm long x 36"/91.4 wide

Skill Level Easy

Wool Weight

- *various*

Materials

- Approx 500 yds/458m of bulky yarn (Yarn Standard #5) color White (A)
- Approx 2000 yds/1829m of 11 other yarns in various colors, textures, and sizes (B)

Tools

- US Size 50 (25mm) 28" (700mm) straight needles
- US Size N/15 (10mm) crochet hook

Gauge

- 4 sts x 4 rows = 4"/10cm in Seed St with 12 strands held tog

Seed Stitch (odd number of stitches)

Row 1 (RS): *K1, P1; rep from * to last st, K1.
Repeat Row 1 for Seed St.

Throw

With 12 strands (1 of A and 11 of B) held together, CO 57 sts.
Work Row 1 of Seed St.
Continue in Seed St until piece measures 36"/91.4cm from CO.
BO all sts at a similar tension to CO edge.

Finishing

Edging
With 1 strand of A and crochet hook, work 1 sc in each stitch or row across all 4 sides.
Join to beginning and fasten off.
Weave in ends.

No one will believe this
eye-catching sash is as easy
as this, made with stash
yarns from your collection.

- Obi is sized to fit Women's Small (Medium, Large, X-Large).

Finished Measurements
- Waist 28 (34, 38, 42)"/71.1 (86.4, 96.5, 106.7)cm
- Width 5½"/14cm

Skill Level Beginner

Wool Weight
- Yarn Standard #3 & #4

Materials
- 80 yds/74m each of 4 DK weight yarns (Yarn Standard #3)
- 80 yds/74m each of 2 worsted weight yarns (Yarn Standard #4)
- 80 yds/74m each of 2 worsted weight ribbons (Yarn Standard #4)

Tools
- Size 35 US (19mm) 16" (400mm) straight needles
- Size N/15 US (10mm) crochet hook

Gauge
- 5 sts x 8 rows = 4"/10cm in Seed St holding 8 strands tog

Designer Notes
- Total length of knitted piece is approx 27"/68.6cm long, but is not meant to circle the waist and meet. The ties account for the remaining length.

Seed Stitch (odd number of stitches)

Row 1 (RS): *K1, P1; rep from * to last st, K1.
Repeat Row 1 for Seed St.

Obi

With 8 strands held tog, CO 7 sts, leaving a 12"/30.5cm tail.
Work Row 1 of Seed St.
Continue in Seed St until piece measures 27"/68.6cm from CO.
BO all sts, leaving a 12"/30.5cm tail.

Finishing

Closure
With 8 strands held tog, cut (22) 24"/61cm lengths of fringe. With crochet hook, lay fringe evenly over hook in groups of 4, align the tails, pull hook through edge, and then insert tails through loop. Attach fringe in groups of 4 to bind off and cast on edges in 6 places: beg and end of bind off row, beg and end of cast on row, center of bind off row, center of cast on row.
Note: Incorporate cast on tails and bind off tails into fringe.

To facilitate tying and securing of belt while wearing, place two knots in each group of fringe fibers. Position the first knot approximately 4"/10cm from cast on/bind off edge. Second knot should be placed 4"/10cm below the first knot.

A circle is the reflection of eternity.
It has no beginning and it has no end,
and if you put several circles over each
other, then you get a spiral.

Maynard J. Keenan (1964 –)

Chapter 3
Double Points and Marvelous I-Cords

**Size 8 US (5mm), Size 11 US (8mm), Size 30 US (19mm), Size 50 US (25mm)
double pointed needles**

Double-pointed needles are traditionally used for knitting socks, mittens, and hats. Usually you need four or five of them to work in the round. However, with just two of these needles, you can make an I-Cord that can be adapted to a variety of creative uses.

I-Cords are actually knitted tubes or cords. They are very easy to knit. According to *Knitter's Handbook* by Montse Stanley, the name *I-Cord* is a polite abbreviation for "idiot cord," but I prefer to think of it as *inspirational cord*.

Here are just a few examples of how to use I-Cords: shoulder straps for a garment, handles for a bag, headbands, necklaces, belts, rugs, surface embellishments, and trims — the list goes on!

Start by casting on three to six stitches, and knit every row without turning your work. There are many good animations and videos available via the Internet that demonstrate how to make an I-Cord. If you need a hands-on lesson, head to your local yarn shop.

Basic 4-Stitch I-Cord Pattern

CO 4 sts.
*K4, pull tail downwards.
Do not turn the work.
Slide the stitches to other end of needle;
Repeat from * to desired length.
BO all sts.
Remember to pull the tail down after every row or two to set the stitches.

I-Cord Tutorial

Begin by casting on 4 stitches. Leave a tail. It can be used in attaching the I-Cord later.

Step 1
Knit 4 stitches.

Step 2
Pull the tail downwards.

Step 3
Do not turn work. Slide the sts to other end of needle.

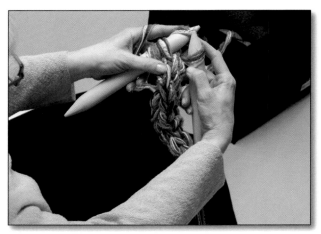

Step 4
Pull working yarn tight and K4 sts.

Once desired length has been reached, bind off using the method described next.

Binding Off

Use the same method when binding off an I-Cord as you would to bind off with regular needles. Knit two stitches and pull the first stitch over the second one. Knit another stitch and repeat the process. Break the yarn, pass the tail through the last stitch, and tighten. By forming this knot, the piece will hold together.

Changing Yarns

You can change yarns as you work your I-Cord, substituting colors or textures. Just make sure that the new yarn you attach is the same weight as the previous one. This will ensure that your gauge will remain the same, and the I-Cord will maintain its shape.

A Family Affair

Unlike knitting on straight needles where an even gauge is very important, a large I-Cord project can be shared by the whole family. Everyone can make a few rows along the way. Be careful that the stitches do not fall off the needle. Ripping back or un-knitting a few rows can be tricky, especially if you are new to this technique.

Ideas for Big Stitch I-Cord Projects

- Rugs
- Pillows
- Cushions
- Belts
- Large bows
- Straps and gussets for tote bags or purses

A playful piece for
your child's room.

Finished Measurements

- 47"/119.4cm diameter

Skill Level Easy

Wool Weight

- *Various*

Materials

- 150 yds/138m of 6 sport weight or larger yarns, color group Red (A)
- 225 yds/206m of 6 sport weight or larger yarns, color group Orange (B)
- 300 yds/275m of 6 sport weight or larger yarns, color group Yellow (C)
- 325 yds/298m of 6 sport weight or larger yarns, color group Blue (D)
- 525 yds/480m of 6 sport weight or larger yarns, color group Purple (E)
- Smooth non-cotton yarn to sew rug together and attach backing
- 60" x 60" (152.4cm x 152.4 cm) **The BagSmith** mesh netting (for backing)

Tools

- Size 50 US (25mm) double pointed needles
- Tapestry needle or curved needle

Gauge

- 4 sts x 4 rows = 4"/10cm in Stockinette St with 6 strands held tog

Designer Notes

- To create a gradient effect, yarns should be joined one at a time over several rows while making the I-Cord. Be sure to join similar weight yarns to one another. For example, sport weight Orange (B) replaces sport weight Red (A).
- The nylon mesh netting will allow the rug to be washed as necessary. If you plan to wash the rug, make sure your fibers are machine washable.

Rug

Make 3-Stitch I-Cord

With 6 strands of A held together, CO 3 sts.
*K3, slide sts to RH side of ndl without turning, and pull working yarn downwards; rep from *.
Work even with A until I-Cord measures approx 6½ yds (6.0m) from CO.
Over the next several rows, join B to A, replacing one strand at a time, and work even until I-Cord measures approximately 12½ yds (11.5m) from CO.
As above, join C to B and work even until I-Cord measures approximately 21½ yds (19.7m) from CO.
Join D to C as above, and work even until I-Cord measures approximately 31½ yds (28.8m) from CO.
Join E to D as above and work even until I-Cord measures approximately 46 yds (42m) from CO.
BO all sts.

Finishing

Beg with cast on end (A), shape the I-Cord into a spiral-shaped coil on a large, flat space. Keep in mind that you are looking at the BACK of the rug.
Place mesh netting on top of coil.
With tapestry needle or curved needle and 1 strand of a smooth non-cotton yarn, sew netting to coil securely, spacing sewn stitches approximately 1"/2.5cm apart.
Carefully cut away excess netting.

Back of rug closeup for finishing

Finished Measurements

- 38"/96.5cm diameter

Skill Level Easy

Wool Weight

- *Various*

Materials

- 400 yds/366m of 6 sport weight or larger yarns, color group Black (A)
- 400 yds/366m of 6 sport weight or larger yarns, color group White (B)
- 48" x 48" (122cm x 122cm) nylon mesh netting (for backing)

Tools

- Size 50 US (25mm) double pointed needles
- Tapestry needle or curved needle

Gauge

- 4 sts x 4 rows = 4"/10cm in Stockinette St with 6 strands held tog

Designer Notes

- The nylon mesh netting will allow the rug to be washed as necessary. If you plan to wash the rug, make sure your fibers are machine washable.

Rug

Make 3-Stitch I-Cord
With 4 strands of A and 2 strands of B held together, CO 3 sts.
*K3, slide sts to RH side of ndl without turning, and pull working yarn downwards; rep from * until I-Cord measures approximately 3 yds (2.75m) from CO.
Mixing strands of A and B at random, work even until I-Cord measures approximately 23 yds (21m) from CO.
With 4 strands of A and 2 strands of B, work even until I-Cord measures approximately 27 yds (24.7m) from CO.
BO all sts.

Finishing

Beg with cast on end (A), shape the I-Cord into a spiral-shaped coil on a large, flat space. Keep in mind that you are looking at the BACK of the rug. Place mesh netting on top of coil. With tapestry needle or curved needle and 1 strand of a smooth non-cotton yarn, sew netting to coil securely, spacing sewn stitches approximately 1"/2.5cm apart.
Carefully cut away excess netting.

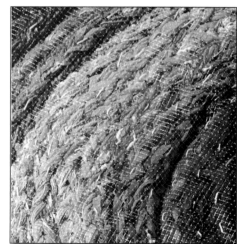

Back of rug closeup for finishing

Freshen the look and extend the life of your favorite indoor or outdoor bench with this attractive and comfortable cushion pair made with a simple I-Cord.

I-Cord Bench Seat Cushions

Finished Measurements

- Bench Seat Cushion 41"/104cm (left to right) x 18"/45.7cm (front to back)
- Bench Back Cushion 39"/99cm (left to right) x 13"/33cm (top to seat)

Skill Level Easy

Wool Weight

- *Yarn Standard #5*

Materials

- **Seat Cushion:** 24, 100g (132 yd/121m) skeins **Noro** *Silver Thaw* (50% wool, 25% angora, 25% nylon) color #9 (MC)
- **Back Cushion:** 12, 100g (132 yd/121m) skeins **Noro** *Silver Thaw* (50% wool, 25% angora, 25% nylon) color #9 (MC)
- Worsted weight yarn in complementary color (cushion ties)

Tools

- Size US 50 (25mm) double pointed needles
- Size US 50 (25mm) 32" (800mm) straight needles
- Size I/9 US crochet hook
- Darning needle

Gauge

- 4 sts x 4 rows = 4"/10cm in Stockinette St with 6 strands of MC held tog

Designer Notes

- The cushions in this pattern are designed for a specific garden bench. See end of this pattern for making a cushion to fit your bench or chair.
- Before cushions are worked, it will be necessary to create the I-Cord, which then becomes the "yarn" to make the seat cushions. Follow the directions at the beginning of this chapter for how to make the I-Cord.

Bench Seat Cushion

With 6 strands of MC held together and dpns, work 4-Stitch I-Cord to a minimum length of 90 yds (82.3m). Wrap I-Cord into a large ball.
With straight ndls and finished I-Cord, CO 24 sts.
Row 1 (RS): Knit.
Continue even in Garter St until piece measures 18" (45.7cm).
BO all sts.

Finishing

Unravel any remaining I-Cord (of a substantial amount), then BO these sts and secure ends into piece.

Cushion Ties

With crochet hook and 2 strands of worsted weight yarn, ch 12, leaving a 12" (30.5cm) tail at both ends. Make 5 more lengths of chain in the same manner. Attach ties to cushion at four corners and two more points evenly spaced across the back. Tie seat cushion to rungs on bench.

Bench Back Cushion

With 6 strands of MC held together and dpns, work 4-Stitch I-Cord until all required yarn has been used.
Wrap I-Cord into a large ball.
With straight ndls and finished I-Cord, CO 8 sts.
Row 1 (RS): Knit.
Continue even in Garter St until piece measures 39"/99m from CO.
BO all sts.

Finishing

Finish as for Bench Seat Cushion.

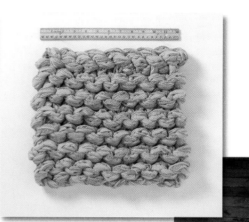

Make It Your Own!

Try making a 12" x 12"/30.5cm x 30.5cm seat pillow to stow in the car, spruce up the patio furniture, or have a great cushion at the ballgame.

Materials

- 25 yds/23m of 7 DK weight or larger yarns (Yarn Standard #3, #4, #5)

Make the I-Cord

With Size 50 US (25mm) double pointed ndls and 7 strands held together, CO 3 sts and work the I-Cord until piece measures 19 yds (17.4m) from CO. BO all sts.

Make the Seat Pillow

With Size 50 US (25mm) straight ndls and the I-Cord, CO 8 sts. Work in Garter St for 14 rows.
BO all sts.
Weave in ends, and take it on the go!

"And what is the Scientific Community doing

about these problems, young people?

THEY'RE CLONING SHEEP. Great! Just what we need!

Sheep that look MORE ALIKE than they already do!

Thanks a lot, Scientific Community!"

Dave Barry (1947 –   )

Chapter 4
Wrap the Roving

About Wool Roving and Top

Most of us knit with wool or other fibers that have been spun into yarn. We rarely think about the original source of the raw material. The next few patterns in this chapter use wool in a form that is not spun. It is known as "top." Knitting with top on the big needles gives a lush fabric, great for rugs, belts, and purses.

There are many animal fibers available in roving and top. Fibers include a wide variety of sheep, llamas, goats, rabbits, camels, and silk. Wool fibers are evaluated based on a number of factors including color, staple length (the length of the wool fibers) and crimp (the kinks or waves in the wool fiber).

Roving and top are usually sold by the ounce or pound, and the prices vary greatly depending on the type of fiber and the animal it comes from. There are many resources for purchasing top and roving on the Internet. Just search the topic "roving and top" and a long list will appear.

If you have the time, attend one of the many sheep and wool festivals that take place from the spring through the summer and fall. These events are wonderful and are great resources for yarn, roving, and top produced by local farms. Many dye their own wool, and you can speak directly with the sheep's owners!

Here are a few definitions that will be helpful when buying the material you need for the patterns in this chapter:

Roving is a long piece, about two to four inches in diameter, with the fibers in random directions.

Top is a long piece like roving and is sometimes referred to as *worsted top*. Unlike roving, top is prepared by combing, which keeps the wool fibers parallel to each other.

Batts are wool fibers that are spread out flat in random directions in a wide format. It is usually fairly thin in depth and can be a few or many inches wide and long. Batts are commonly used for needle felting and for making large, flat pieces of felt.

Carding is the process of brushing raw or washed fibers. This is how the fibers are prepared for spinning yarn. Tangles are eliminated in this process. Woolen yarns are spun from carded fiber.

Combing is the process for preparing the fiber for spinning using combs. The combs have long metal teeth and two are used at the same time. This process removes the short fibers and arranges the fiber in a flat bundle with all of the fibers running in the same direction. It is used for the preparation of worsted yarn.

Wrap the Roving

The technique of "wrapping the roving" secures and contains the fibers that would normally occur when spinning and twisting the yarn. Roving can be wrapped with any type of #0, #1, or #2 yarns, ribbons, or metallic blending filaments, just to name a few types.

You may discover that wrapping the roving takes as much or more time than subsequent knitting, but you will find that it adds a great deal to the final look of your piece. Try a few different combinations before wrapping all of your roving.

Divide the Roving or Top

Roving or top is soft and usually available in approximately a 1"/2.5cm diameter core. This is quite thick to knit, even with a Size 50 US (25mm) needle. The patterns that follow indicate how to divide the roving into smaller sections.

Follow the instructions in each pattern for dividing the roving. In some cases, only half the thickness is used. In other cases, a quarter (half of the half) of the thickness is used. The trick is to divide the roving as evenly and consistently as possible to maintain an even working gauge.

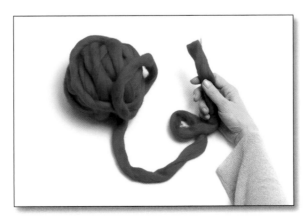

Step 1: Roving or top

Step 2: Divide the roving

Wrap It!
Once the roving has been divided, begin to wrap the roving with the commercial yarn in 1" (2.5cm) sections. Wind wrapped roving into a ball.

Step 3: Wrap the roving

Make It Your Own!

Other project ideas for roving include a scarf, coat, throw, pillow, or seat cushion.

This is a fun project that takes less time to knit than it does to prepare the roving.

Wrapped Roving I-Cord Belt

Sizes
- Belt is sized to fit Women's Small (Medium, Large, X-Large).

Finished Measurements
- Waist 38 (42, 46, 50)"/96.5 (106.7, 116.8, 127)cm

Skill Level Beginner

Wool Weight
- *Yarn Standard #5*

Materials
- 8 oz (227g) **Fiberlicious** *100% Merino Wool Roving* color Natural
- 1, 150 yd/138m skein **The Great Adirondack Yarn Co.** *Surprise* (70% rayon, 25% cotton, 5% polyester) color Mango (A)

Tools
- Size 35 US (19mm) double pointed needles

Gauge
- 4 sts x 4 rows = 4"/10cm in Stockinette St

Designer Notes
- Make belt longer (and wider, if desired) to wear around hips.

Prepare the Roving

Divide roving in half and then divide each piece in half (4 pieces out of the length). With A and a length of roving, secure A by wrapping the roving several times at start and knot. Continue across first length, wrapping roving tightly with A in 1"/2.5cm sections. To join the next length of roving, overlap the end of the wrapped length to the beginning of the unwrapped length. Wrap A around the roving several times and knot, but do not cut A. Continue wrapping until entire length of all 4 pieces has been wrapped. Fasten off A. Wind roving into a ball.

Belt

With 1 strand of wrapped roving and dpns, CO 3 sts, leaving a 12"/30.5cm tail.
Work 3-Stitch I-Cord (see Chapter 3) until piece meaures 38 (42, 46, 48)"/96.5 (106.7, 116.8, 127)cm.
BO all sts, leaving a 12"/30.5cm tail.

Finishing

Belt should be felted slightly in order to prevent shedding. Wearing rubber gloves for comfort, place the finished belt in a tub of hot water with some dish soap or wool wash. Allow the belt to soak for 5 minutes, agitating it slightly until the fibers just begin to felt. Transfer the belt to a basin of cold water, mixed with a capful of white vinegar (to remove the soap). Dry flat, and add embellishments like tassels and beads as desired.

Back of bag

Here is a dramatic new take on an old favorite. Take it to the beach, take it shopping, take it everywhere!

Finished Measurements

- 12"/30.5cm tall x 18"/45.7cm wide x 2"/5.1cm deep

Skill Level Easy

Wool Weight

- *Yarn Standard #3, #4 & #5*

Materials

- 2 lbs (1 kilo) **Brown Sheep** *Top of the Lamb (roving)* (100% wool) color Turquoise
- 1, 50g (205 yd/188m) ball **Ironstone Yarns** *Paris Nights* (67% acrylic, 12% metal, 21% nylon) color #21 Pirate (A)
- 1 spool (43 yd/40m) **The BagSmith** *Sumptuous Silk Ribbon* (100% Silk) color Glacier Martini (to attach liner)
- 1, **The BagSmith** *Extreme Purse Liner*, Item #6051W
- 1, purse closure, **Artistic Visions / Cristine Hines**, item Paisley Purse Closure
- DK weight scrap yarn in a complementary color (to attach closure)

Tools

- Size 35 US (19mm) 20" (500mm) straight needles
- Size U US (25mm) crochet hook
- Darning needle

Gauge

- 4 sts x 8 rows= 4"/10cm in Garter St

Prepare the Roving

Divide roving in half. With A and a length of roving, secure A by wrapping the roving several times at start and knot. Continue across first length, wrapping roving tightly with A in 1"/2.5cm sections. To join the next length of roving, overlap the end of the wrapped length to the beginning of the unwrapped length, and wrap A around the roving several times and knot, but do not cut A. Continue wrapping until entire length of each piece has been wrapped. Fasten off A. Wind roving into a ball.

Handbag

Body
With wrapped roving, CO 18 sts.
Row 1 (RS): Knit.
Continue even in Garter St until piece measures 26"/23.8cm from CO.
BO 17 sts, leaving last loop on ndl.
Do not break yarn.

Shoulder Strap
Insert crochet hook into last loop and make a 30"/27.4cm chain. Fold bag in half so that bind off edge meets cast on edge. Making sure that the chain is not twisted, insert hook through Front and Back of bag at opposite corner and work 1 sc into corner.

Join Side Seams
With wrapped roving and crochet hook, join side seam by working 1 row sc to bottom edge. Fasten off and weave in roving end. Join roving at opposite open corner and work 1 row sc to close side seam as for other side.

Loop Closure
With wrapped roving and crochet hook, ch 17 and fasten off. Attach and center chain to inside (WS) of Back about 2"/1.8cm from open edge. Secure tightly in place. Attach glass closure to the middle of the chain with scrap DK yarn and darning ndl. Attach snap fastener for closure on outside Front (RS) opposite the glass piece.

Install Liner
Place purse liner inside finished bag, being sure closure is attached before inserting liner. With *Silk Ribbon* and darning ndl, whipstitch liner in place, drawing darning ndl through grommets on liner. Secure all ends.

BagSmith Extreme Purse Liner

Soft, gorgeous roving is wrapped with a wool yarn, keeping the fibers in place for easy knitting in this piece.

Finished Measurements

- 42"/38.4cm long x 30"/27.4cm wide

Skill Level Easy

Wool Weight

- Yarn Standard #6

Materials

- 5 lbs (2.3 kilo) **Fiberlicious** *100% Merino Wool Roving* color Natural
- 2, (150 yd/138m) skeins **Fiberlicious** *Oh So Soft* (wool, alpaca, mohair) color Pink Lady (CC)

Tools

- Size 50 (25mm) 28" (700mm) straight needles

Gauge

- 4 sts x 5 rows = 4"/10cm in Stockinette St using wrapped roving

Prepare the Roving

Divide roving in half. With A and a length of roving, secure A by wrapping the roving several times at start and knot. Continue across first length, wrapping roving tightly with A in 1"/2.5cm sections. To join the next length of roving, overlap the end of the wrapped length to the beginning of the unwrapped length. Wrap A around the roving several times and knot but do not cut A. Continue wrapping until entire length of each piece has been wrapped. Fasten off A. Wind roving into a ball.

Rug

With 1 strand of wrapped roving, CO 30 sts.
Row 1 (RS): Knit.
Continue even in Stockinette St until piece measures 42"/106.7cm from CO, end after working a WS row.
BO all sts.
Weave in ends.

Finishing

Rug should be felted slightly in order to prevent shedding. Wearing rubber gloves for comfort, place the finished rug in a tub of hot water, with some dish soap or wool wash. Allow the rug to soak for 5 minutes, agitating it slightly until the fibers just begin to felt. Transfer the rug to a basin of cold water, mixed with a capful of white vinegar. Place the rug in the dryer for a ½ hour on medium heat to remove excess moisture then lay flat until completely dry.

Make It Your Own!

The possibilities here are endless. Try using a variety of colors of roving with varying wool yarns for the wrapping. Try different stitches. We found that the simple ones are easiest to use because of the thickness of the fiber.

"*More is never enough.*"
Miss Piggy

Chapter 5
Free Range Fibers

Embellishments can add texture, color interest, and eye-catching appeal to your knitting. Whether it is a simple crocheted edge or a freeform flourish, embellishments can transform a pattern from a book into a personal statement.

Using a variety of sizes in both knitting needles and crochet hooks can give you tremendous options, from long I-Cords sewn in the shape of a swirl on a pillow, to big stitch collars, to flowers in graduated sizes on the front of a sweater.

Embellishing your work gives you the opportunity to play and to improvise. There are no rules. You can make many shapes and then decide to use only one or maybe a few. You can change fibers, colors, stitches, and shapes. The idea is to experiment and enjoy the process.

Some people can jump right into this area of knitting while others are a bit more timid, not knowing exactly how to begin. Here are a few improvisations that can break the creative ice for you.

Improvisation #1 - A Freeform Shape

Begin with Size 10 US (6mm) or Size 10.5 US (6.5mm) straight or circular needles and cast on 9 stitches using a worsted weight yarn. Knit the first 2 rows. Next row: decrease one stitch at each end of the needle on the next row. Knit one row. Repeat the decrease row and the knit row once more. You should have 5 sts. Now increase one stitch at the beginning of the next row. Knit one row and repeat the last two rows until your 9 stitches are back on the needle. Knit two rows.

Take a Size I crochet hook and bind off using the crochet hook. When you arrive at the final stitch, change yarns. You can use a thinner or thicker yarn and adjust the size of the hook accordingly. Now single crochet all around the bow shape that you knitted. When you arrive at the beginning of the single crochet row, chain 11 and begin making another shape. If you do not want to crochet the next shape, use the loop as the first stitch on the needle and cast on 10 more stitches.

For those who do not know how to crochet, a similar effect can be obtained by whipstitching around the shape using a contrasting yarn and a large eye darning needle.

Improvisation #2 - Basic Flower Shapes

Here is the pattern for a basic flower shape. Try it using Size 9 US (5.5mm) needles and a single strand of yarn. When trying this shape on Size 15 US (10mm) needles, use two strands of yarn and with the Size 50 US (25mm) needles, use five fibers together.

Cast on 15 sts and knit 1 row. Next row: knit into front and back of each stitch [30 sts]. Repeat last row. Bind off all stitches. You will have a long piece of knitted fabric that will ruffle. Twist it into a flower shape and stitch in place.

Improvisation #3 - Noodles

With a Size S US (19mm) crochet hook and three yarns of varying weights, chain 8 and connect the chain together, making a circle. Single crochet around the circle again and again. Change yarns at will, making new combinations as you go. You can make your noodle as long as you like. Once you decide where to use it, fill it with fiber, beads, shells, mohair locks, or whatever you like!

References

There are many wonderful books on the market exploring embellishments and freeform knitting that can serve as a resource. It is great fun to explore shapes, textures, and knit and crochet techniques. Here are a few resources:

Knitted Embellishments:
350 Appliqués, Borders,
Cords, and More!
by Nicky Epstein
ISBN: 1-883010-39-X
272 pages
Published by Interweave Press

Freeform Knitting and Crochet
by Jenny Dowde
ISBN: 1-86351-327-2
176 pages
Published by Sally Milner Publishing

Freeform: Serendipitous
Design Techniques
for Knitting & Crochet
by Prudence Mapstone
ISBN: 0-9580443-0-9
87 pages
Published by Prudence Mapstone

Contemporary Knitting
for Textile Artists
by Ruth Lee
ISBN–13: 9780713490466
125 pages
First published in the United Kingdom in 2007 by Batsford.
Distributed in the US and Canada by Sterling Publishing Co.

This project is a jump
off from the
Stashionista Wall
Hanging. Start there
and let your
imagination run wild!

Finished Measurements

- 45"/114.3cm long x 25"/63.5cm wide

Skill Level Experienced

Wool Weight

- Yarn Standard #3, #4 & #5

Materials

- 60 yds/55m of 12 DK weight or larger yarns, color group Black (A)
- 60 yds/55m of 12 DK weight or larger yarns, color group Dark Brown (B)
- 60 yds/55m of 12 DK weight or larger yarns, color group Medium Brown (C)
- 60 yds/55m of 12 DK weight or larger yarns, color group Orange (D)
- 60 yds/55m of 12 DK weight or larger yarns, color group Gold/Beige (E)
- 1, 32" curtain rod, flagpole, or dowel rod and appropriate hardware to hang the piece.

Tools

- Size 35 US (19mm) 24" (600mm) straight needles
- Assorted Size F (4mm) to S (19mm) crochet hooks
- Assorted Size 7 (4.5mm) to 11 (8mm) needles
- Large eye darning needle

Gauge

- 5 sts x 7 rows = 4"/10cm in Seed St, with 12 strands held together

Designer Notes

- Vary the yarn weights over DK, worsted, and bulky within color groups.
- Additional yarns, including metallics and other novelties, can be used in the freeform sections.
- Once hung, piece may stretch depending on length, yarns used, and density of stitches.
- The denser the knitted fabric, the less significantly it will stretch.

Seed Stitch (odd number of stitches)

Row 1 (RS): *K1, P1; rep from * to last st, K1.
Repeat Row 1 for Seed St.

Wall Hanging

With 12 strands from darkest color group (A), CO 31 sts.
Work Row 1 of Seed St.
Continue in Seed St until piece measures approximately 6"/15.2cm.
Continue in Seed St as established, and begin next color group (B) by replacing 2 yarns every row over the next 6 rows with 2 new (B) yarns. When all strands from (A) have been exchanged for new color group (B), work even in Seed St and color group (B) for approximately 3"/7.6cm.
Rep from * to * until all groups have been incorporated.

Rod Pocket

Work even in Seed St for an additional 3"/7.6cm.
BO all sts.
Fold bind off edge over to WS, creating a 3"/7.6cm rod pocket. With darning needle and a worsted weight yarn from color group E, sew bind off edge to WS, leaving side edges open.

Freeform Embellishment

The sample demonstrates the author's improvisation. Elements were not planned ahead, but were worked both directly on the piece and in separate pieces that were sewn on later. Experiment! You can choose to work directly into the knitted hanging with a crochet hook and yarn, or you can create knitted or crocheted shapes to attach.

Instructions for two of the embellishments are featured below. Also refer to the improvisation exercises at the beginning of this chapter.

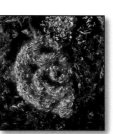

Orange Block

With Trendsetter Yarns *Aura* and needles of your choice, CO 20 sts.
Row 1 (RS): Knit.
Continue even in St st until desired length or a square has been achieved.
BO all sts.
With darning needle and 1 strand of yarn, embroider or sew shapes onto the knitted fabric. Attach to the wall hanging.

Wavy Shapes

With Size 10 US (6mm) ndls and yarn of your choice, CO 80 sts.
Row 1 (RS): Knit.
Continue even in St st until piece measures 3"/7.6cm.
BO all sts evenly and weave in ends.
Sew or crochet shape to wall hanging, forming waves or other shapes and stitch the knitted fabric in place.
To further embellish with a contrasting color of yarn and crochet hook, sc into the top edge of the shape and work to end of shape.
Fasten off.

Finishing

Weave in all ends. Slip pole through rod pocket and attach to wall.

Resources

Tools

Rachel John's Extreme Needles©
Worldwide:
The BagSmith®
20600 Chagrin Blvd STE 101
Shaker Heights, OH 44122
216.921.3500
www.bagsmith.com

Europe & UK:
Rachel John, Textile Artist
Borough Farm, Castle Street
King's Stanley GL10 3TX
England, United Kingdom
www.racheljohn.co.uk

Big Stitch©
Double Pointed Needles
Big Stitch© Crochet Hooks
The BagSmith®
20600 Chagrin Blvd STE 101
Shaker Heights, OH 44122
216.921.3500
www.bagsmith.com

Purse Liners, Rug Backing, Yarn Catchers
The BagSmith®
20600 Chagrin Blvd STE 101
Shaker Heights, OH 44122
216.921.3500
www.bagsmith.com

Embellishments

Artistic Visions / Cristine Hynes
112 Spears Creek Dr
Mooresville, NC 28117
704.660.8085
www.artisticvisionsdesign.com
(Elegant Carpet Bag)

Muench Yarns, Inc.
285 Bel Marin Keys Blvd UNIT J
Novato, CA 94949-5763
800.733.9276
www.muenchyarns.com
(Summer Love Beach Bag)

Original Artworx / Bonnie Tuscano
P.O. Box 3396
Tequesta, FL 33469
561.744.5501
www.originalartworx.com
(Big Easy Jacket)

Yarn

AslanTrends
8 Maple St
Port Washington, NY 11050
800.314.8202
www.aslantrends.com
(Big Easy Jacket)

Bernat Yarns
320 Livingstone Ave S
Listowel, ON N4W 3H3
Canada
888.368.8401
www.bernat.com
(Simple Pocket Scarf)

Berroco, Inc.
P.O. Box 367
Uxbridge, MA 01569
508.278.2527
www.berroco.com
(Caribbean Sea Afghan)

Brown Sheep Company, Inc.
100662 County Road 16
Mitchell, NE 69357
800.826.9136
www.brownsheep.com
(Elegant Carpet Bag)

Below you will find a list of manufacturers and distributors of the yarns and supplies listed in the book. Most of them have websites where they list the local yarn shops (LYS) where their goods are sold. Your LYS is a great resource and a place to play with different fiber combinations for the stashionista projects. Support your local yarn shop!

Decadent Fibers
www.decadentfibers.com
(The Cuddle)

Fiberlicious
8157 Camargo Rd
Madeira, OH 45243
513.561.8808
www.fiberlicious.com
(Wrapped Roving Rug)

Fiesta Yarns
Ironstone Yarns
5401 San Diego NE
Albuquerque, NM 87113
505.892.5008
www.fiestayarns.com
(Big Easy Jacket, Wrapped Roving Rug)

The Great Adirondack Yarn Company
950 County Highway 126
Amsterdam, NY 12010
518.843.3381
For shop locations visit:
www.knitting.com
(Raspberry Sensation Tote)

Noro Yarns /
Knitting Fever Inc: (KFI)
P.O. Box 336
Amityville, NY 11701
561.546.3600
www.knittingfever.com
(Bench Seat Cushions)

Oasis Yarn
DJ International, Inc.
35 Second Ave.
Berea, OH 44017
440.260.7593
www.oasisyarn.com
(Raspberry Sensation Tote)

Pagewood Farm
San Pedro, CA
310.403.7880
www.pagewoodfarm.com
(Woolly Vest, Skirt, and Sarong)

Trendsetter Yarns
16745 Saticoy St STE 101
Van Nuys, CA 91406
818.780.5497
www.trendsetteryarns.com
(Barrel Pillow, Wildflower Top)

Stitch Glossary

approx	approximately
beg	begin
BO	bind off
ch	chain
CO	cast on
dpn(s)	double pointed needle(s)
foll	follows
inc	increase
K	knit
K2tog	knit 2 stitches together (1 stitch decrease)
kwise	knitwise
LH	left hand
m	marker
ndl(s)	needle(s)
P	purl
P2tog	purl 2 stitches together (1 stitch decrease)
P2togtbl	purl 2 stitches together through the back loop (1 stitch decrease)
patt	pattern
pm	place marker
PM	place marker
pwise	purlwise
Rep	repeat
RH	right hand
rnd	round
RS	right side
sc	single crochet
sk	skip
slm	slip marker
ssk	slip, slip, knit these 2 stitches together (1 stitch decrease)
St	stitch
st(s)	stitch(es)
tog	together
WS	wrong side
wyib	with yarn in back
wyif	with yarn in front
yds	yards
yo	yarn over

Becca Smith

Becca Smith is a lifelong and passionate knitter who loves working with great fibers. She juggles many roles as a wife, mother, daughter, and business owner. She is Vice President of two family-owned businesses, Smith International Enterprises, Inc. (www.smithintl.com), an international trading company, and H C Smith Ltd. (www.hcsmith.com), a retained executive search firm, both located in Cleveland, Ohio.

As part of her role at Smith International, Ms. Smith created The BagSmith®, a supplier of unique and innovative products to independent yarn shops in the United States and abroad. Patterns and designs are created in-house at The BagSmith®. Television guest appearances include the Shay Pendray Needle Arts Studio Show on PBS and Knitting Daily, also on PBS. Currently, The BagSmith® supplies more than 800 stores in the United States, Canada, the United Kingdom, and France. All of the products can be seen on their award-winning website: www.bagsmith.com. More information about Big Stitch Knitting can be found on www.bigstitchknitting.com.

Ms. Smith earned a B.M. Ed. and an M.M. Ed. from Chicago Musical College and a Master of Philosophy in Teaching Humanities at Roosevelt University. She was named EPDA Fellow in 1971. She was a founder and director of the Master's in Interdisciplinary Arts at Columbia College in Chicago and previously served as Director of Education for The Cleveland Orchestra. She resides in the Cleveland area with her husband, Herb, son, E.B., and Sugar Magnolia, her four-legged knitting and exercise companion. In addition to knitting and crocheting, her interests include traveling and the visual and performing arts.